THE NEW
MIDDLE EAST

THE NEW MIDDLE EAST

Shimon Peres
with Arye Naor

HENRY HOLT AND COMPANY / NEW YORK

Henry Holt and Company, Inc.
Publishers since 1866
115 West 18th Street
New York, New York 10011

Henry Holt® is a registered
trademark of Henry Holt and Company, Inc.

Published in Canada by Fitzhenry & Whiteside Ltd.,
195 Allstate Parkway, Markham, Ontario L3R 4T8.

Library of Congress Cataloging-in-Publication Data
Peres, Shimon.
The New Middle East / Shimon Peres with Arye Naor. — 1st ed.
p.   cm.
Includes bibliographical references.
1. Jewish-Arab relations.   2. Israel-Arab conflicts.   3. Palestinian
Arabs—Politics and government.   4. Middle East—Politics and
government—1979–   .   5. Middle East—Economic integration.
6. Regional planning—Middle East.   7. Declaration of Principles
on Interim Self-Government Arrangements (1993)
I. Naor, Arye.   II. Title.
DS119.7.P447   1993   93-41537
956.05'3—dc20   CIP

ISBN 0-8050-3323-8

Henry Holt books are available for special promotions
and premiums. For details contact:
Director, Special Markets.

First Edition—1993

Translated by Sagir International Translations, Ltd./
G. Ginzach, Jerusalem

Designed by Lucy Albanese

Printed in the United States of America
All first editions are printed on acid-free paper.∞

10 9 8 7 6 5 4 3 2 1

For Michal, Nadav, Noah, Asaf, Guy, Yoel—on their way to the twenty-first century

CONTENTS

THE NEW
MIDDLE EAST

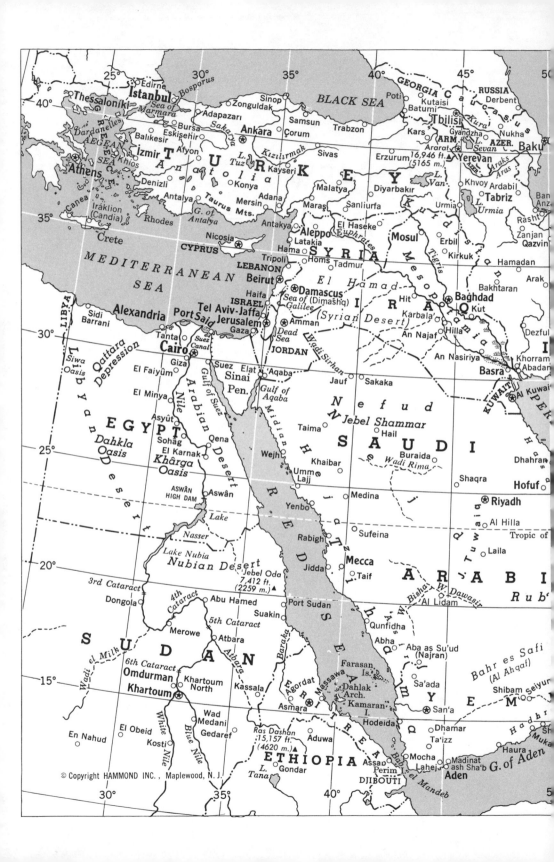

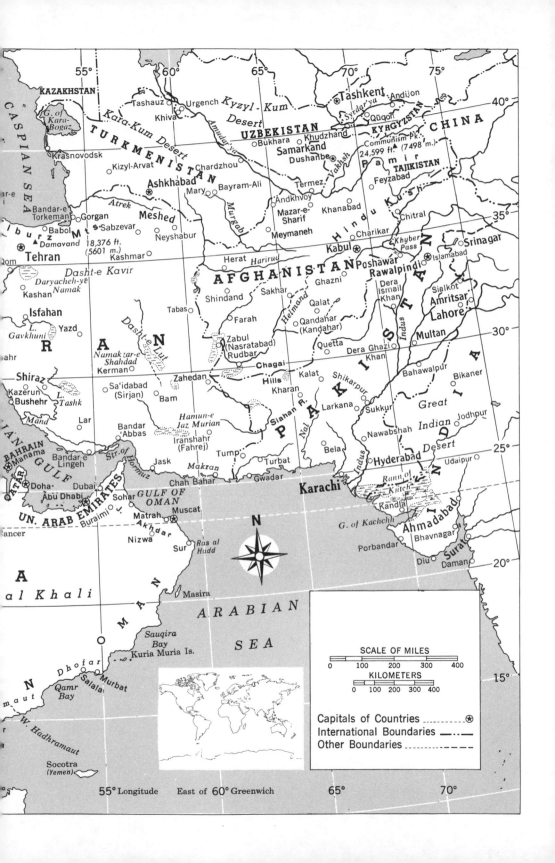

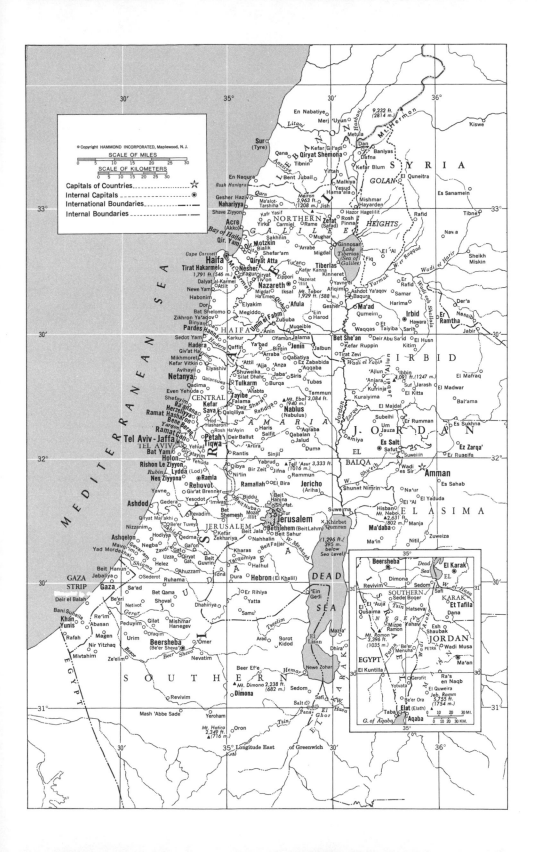

1

THE DAWN
OF PEACE

IT WAS IN THE WEE HOURS OF THE NIGHT,
on August 20, 1993, that the remaining delegates initialed the
finalized document on which we had been working so hard and so
long. An Arab-Israeli accord had at long last been reached.

That night in Oslo I had celebrated my seventieth birthday. In
Israel it was still dark, but in Norway the early northern dawn was
just beginning to show through the mist. Here was a small group
of Israelis, Palestinians, and Norwegians—partners to one of the
best-guarded diplomatic secrets ever, a secret whose imminent
revelation would mark a watershed in the history of the Middle
East.

Abu Alaa, a senior Palestine Liberation Organization (PLO) representative, smiled warmly at me. "This agreement," he said, "is your birthday present."

"And what a present," I thought. "So unique, so unexpected, almost impossible to fathom."

Suddenly I was whisked back in time to the city of my childhood, Vishniva (near Volozhin, now part of Belarus). In those days Vishniva was a center of Jewish spiritual life. Chaim Nachman Bialik, the national poet of Israel, called the great yeshiva of Vishniva a "breeding ground for the Jewish national soul." Today nothing remains of Jewish Vishniva. The synagogues and yeshivas, the businesses and factories—all are gone, destroyed. Jewish life there is a wasteland, a faded memory, like the Jews who once lived there. Had I not left when I did, my fate would have been little different from that of the Jews who were buried in mass graves or sent to their death in gas chambers.

I am a child of the generation that lost one world and went on to build another. We established the modern State of Israel and renewed the independence of the Jewish people in their ancient homeland. But only after the old world had been destroyed and we had taken a long and harrowing journey could we build a new, more just world—a place in which we could unite our yearning for national freedom with our craving for social justice. Sadly, shaping this world also meant terrible wars, suffering, and pain. So much suffering, so much pain that Israelis and Arabs were blinded, making us incapable of changing our images of either "them" or ourselves. That is how opportunities are missed. We were so busy fighting each other that we did not realize how ripe the time was for change.

In the early 1990s, we had reached one of those rare critical junctures that enable discerning statesmen to make a quantum leap in their thinking—and perhaps turn the tide of history. To make the change work, however, we had to open our eyes to the new reality. During those early hours in Oslo I was well aware that, in the half-light of dawn, we had to drive away the shadows of the past. Nighttime fades on its own; the darkness of the past penetrates every component of our lives. But what is done, is done. We cannot change the past. When circumstances are propitious, and so much is at stake, we must forget the past for the sake of the present. But how?

Though we may learn the lessons of history, it is difficult for us to correct our mistakes. The ancient Greek philosopher Heracleitus noted that "Upon those who step into the same river, different and ever different waters flow down." Rivers are in constant flux, their steady flow forever creating a new reality. A man might drown in their waters, but he cannot turn them back. The same holds true for history. We cannot build a future on the ruins of an old order.

Our region has changed dramatically from the days of our forefathers. Abraham, too, knew times of drought and hunger; of fire, wind, and earthquakes; of floods and lost trails—not to mention weapons, war, and bloodshed. But in the days of Abraham people did not have the means to desalinate water, generate electricity, deflect winds, or predict earthquakes. And certainly people knew nothing of missiles, computers, and nuclear warheads.

We must study history to learn its critical lessons, but we must also know when to ignore history. We cannot allow the past to shape immutable concepts that negate our ability to build new roads. Like the river, we are part of the process of perpetual change: landscapes shift, knowledge widens, and technology expands our horizons. Those of us active in the political arena today differ from our predecessors in the burden we carry, in our hopes

and in our expectations. A person who hails historical precedent
as a formula for controlling future events is headed for disap-
pointment and failure. Knowing when to depart from the past
brings a distinct advantage: the element of surprise. Sometimes, in
fact, what comes by surprise generates much less opposition than
what was expected.

Therefore, I have always tried to learn the facts from others
and to imagine the possibilities myself. After the 1948 War of
Independence, Israel still had enemies, but it no longer had weapons. My colleagues and I were assigned the monumental task of
obtaining the arms necessary to defend our new country. While
we were immersed in this effort, I began to perceive things differ-
ently from how I had before independence. What Israel really
needs, I thought, is the strategic capability to deter or intimidate
the enemy—to rid him of his desire for war. My mentor, David
Ben-Gurion, endorsed the idea of a deterrent, with a nuclear gen-
erator to be built in the heart of the desert, in the city of Dimona,
not far from Beersheba. The Dimona project was designed as a
research institute, but in the eyes of neighboring Arabs it became
a worrisome, fuzzy deterrent. At my urging, Israel announced that
it would not introduce nuclear weapons into the Middle East.
Indeed, the plant would arouse hope that there might be a Middle
East without the need for nuclear weapons—a Middle East without war.

The project provoked great controversy in Israel. Some
claimed nothing would come of the plan; others tried to prove it
was not feasible; and still others predicted that, if we took even
one step in this direction, the entire world would rise up against
us and Dimona would drag us into a disastrous war. In 1979,
during the Camp David peace talks with Egypt, one of Anwar el-
Sadat's assistants admitted to then Deputy Prime Minister Yigal

Yadin and to then Defense Minister (today President) Ezer Weizman that Egypt's decision to talk peace had definitely been influenced by the Dimona project.

More than thirty years have elapsed between completion of the Dimona project and my second—even more crucial—opportunity to contribute to the welfare of Israel. By June 1992, with the formation of the new government, the situation was similar: only a few people could see the potential for peace. Israel had come a long way, from a young country that needed Dimona to deter war to a strong nation on the brink of peace. The dream was fulfilled. The vision had become a reality.

AFTER being elected Israeli Prime Minister in 1992, Yitzhak Rabin offered me the cabinet position of Foreign Minister. The job as planned had serious limitations, some of which resulted from the earlier, highly complex relationship between my predecessor, David Levy, and the former Prime Minister, Yitzhak Shamir. Moreover, the previous government had established a fixed and complex mechanism for Arab-Israeli negotiations. Both bilateral and multilateral talks were to take place simultaneously. Israel and three separate Arab delegations—Jordanian-Palestinian, Syrian, and Lebanese—would take part in the bilateral negotiations. The Jordanian-Palestinian delegation later split into two, so that in fact there were now four delegations: three representing those countries, and the fourth (and most complicated, the Palestinian) representing hope.

Only the delegates were present at these face-to-face negotiations. Outside, however, were U.S. State Department officials who worked hard to ensure smooth sailing and encourage the participants to continue amid a storm of turbulent emotions. Meanwhile, the media traced every step the delegates made and documented their every word.

The most complicated negotiation issue was also the most complicated delegation matter: Palestinian representation. The Palestinian population had grown threefold since the end of World War I and the map of the Middle East had changed beyond recognition. A host of organizations were competing for a place at the top of the Palestinian totem pole, some using arms to achieve their goal. To a large degree, the Palestinian delegation to the talks subsequent to the 1991 Madrid Conference was accepted without hesitation. The idea was to have a separate Palestinian leadership that would gain its legitimacy from the fact that Israel was prepared to acquiesce. The delegation was to be composed of only residents of the territories who did not take part in terrorist activities and who had consented to an interim agreement—that is, that the demand to establish a Palestinian state be held in abeyance for at least five years. The delegation was to exclude all representatives of the Palestine Liberation Organization and people from the Palestine National Council. The group was to be totally independent and represent an independent leadership—a leadership, alas, that existed solely in the imagination of the Likud government.

The truth was totally different. The PLO leadership in Tunis pulled the strings: it decided on the composition of the Palestinian delegation, and it appointed Dr. Haddar Abed al-Shafi from Gaza, one of the founders of the PLO, as head of the delegation. The two people who actually ran the delegation weren't even members of it: Faisal Husseini, the uncrowned representative of the PLO in the territories, and Dr. Hanan Ashrawi, its eloquent spokeswoman. In my role as Foreign Minister, I had convened with both of them several times, and I was pleased when Prime

Minister Rabin agreed to officially include Mr. Husseini in the delegation. The directives came, as was apparent to every unbiased observer, from the PLO in Tunis. Gradually, the delegation began to identify publicly with the PLO. Husseini himself termed the relationship of the Palestinian delegation with the PLO leadership as *"fax politica"*—politics via the fax machine. Thus, it turned out that those who determined the course of the talks did not participate in them, whereas those who participated in the talks had no say in the course of the negotiations.

THE bilateral negotiations focused on reconciliation of past differences—borders, territories, water and land rights, security measures—and on a five-year interim Palestinian government. The delegates agreed to postpone discussion of a permanent peace until the third year of autonomy, with talks that would conclude by the end of the fifth year of autonomy. But nevertheless progress was slow.

With Jordan, Israel had a de facto neighborly relationship and no unbridgeable differences of opinion. It was no accident that we reached agreement with the Jordanian delegation on a fixed timetable for peace. Unfortunately, details of the agreement were inadvertently leaked to the press, apparently by the Jordanians, and they were no longer ready to sign. It was assumed that the Jordanians were afraid to be first to take the plunge. In any case, negotiations between the two countries moved rapidly into full gear by May 5, 1993, and had reached the point where the delegates were debating ways to halt the border passage of mosquitoes, which need no visa to sting Jordanians and Israelis indiscriminately.

We also did not have particular difficulties with the Lebanese delegation. Israel has no claim on Lebanese land or to Lebanese sovereignty, and has no desire to play any role in that country's incredibly complex internal politics. Our only desire was for Lebanon to take responsibility for security along its border with Israel, so that terrorists would not use it as a staging area for raids against us. During negotiations we realized that the real problem was not Lebanon's relationship with Israel, but its relationship with Syria. Syria was preventing Lebanon from conducting decisive negotiations as long as the Syrians were making no headway in their talks with Israel.

Words and formulations ran riot during our discussions with the Syrian delegation, which more often than not resembled Talmudic discourse. The Syrians maintained an atmosphere of give-and-take, but refused to descend their mountain of words to the bedrock of reality. They were not ready to specify what kind of peace was being offered—only that they would be satisfied with a peace without ambassadorships—nor what type of security arrangements they were ready to provide. They insisted that Israel first declare its preparedness to withdraw from all occupied territories and vacate all its settlements; only then would they discuss the remaining issues. In short, Syria wanted what Egypt had achieved, at Camp David, but without enduring the lengthy process that led to it—much like the man who wishes to pick his fruit, but has not made the effort to plant or water his trees.

Meanwhile, as negotiations with the Palestinians progressed, the delegates retreated further and further from possible agreement. The talks began to resemble an extended press conference, in which each side takes every opportunity to prove to superiors that it is loyal and constant. The Palestinian delegation was torn to shreds by contradictory, inflexible instructions. Although the PLO did not directly participate in the talks, it outlined the Palestinian position as if the delegation were conducting an ideological discussion with itself.

Palestinians on the street were becoming suspicious. They were more concerned with what the delegation was not getting, not what it had achieved. For the first time, the PLO leadership in Tunis not only became aware of these feelings but took them into consideration. The Palestinian delegation also had to contend with mixed reactions from the larger Arab world, generally reflecting rampant disagreement among its leaders. The PLO's championship of Saddam Hussein during the 1991 Persian Gulf War had cost it, among other things, the financial support of Saudi Arabia. The Saudi Arabians simultaneously approved of the talks and recoiled from them, more because of PLO involvement than because of Israel's position.

Egypt helped as much as it could. It was the only country to which the PLO, Israel, and the United States could turn for assistance at critical junctures. In contrast, Iran did everything in its power to undermine the negotiations. It financed Hamas terrorists, who actively "dealt with" supporters of the peace process. (About 1,000 Palestinians have been killed by their fellow Palestinians, the large majority because of false accusations or unfounded suspicions.) It was also a potent force behind Hizballah in Lebanon, which it used to exploit the internal problems of that country for the ultimate purpose of establishing an Islamic republic that would hurt Israel and Israelis, within the security zone and outside of it.

The United States contributed more than any other country to the success of these negotiations. The Americans set the time and venue for the meetings, and guaranteed that Russia be given its rightful place as co-sponsor. The United States pacified and pressured all sides—as the need arose—to arrive on schedule; it pro-

posed more "diplomatic" wording for draft agreements and even
made tactful threats ("If you don't get on with it, we will pull out
of the talks"). The American representatives were savvy enough
not to take sides during the discussions themselves. Just as the
United States could not serve as a substitute for one of the parties,
the parties themselves could not fill the American role of go-
between.

But even the United States became preoccupied with what is
called in diplomatese the "DOP," or declaration of principles.
The more drafts were perfected, the wider the gap became between the sides. The new, more polished formulations were creating "nays" instead of "ayes." The documents became denser—not
with agreements but with schedules for clarifying nonagreements.

ACCORDING to the division of labor set up by the Prime
Minister and myself, Mr. Rabin was to head the bilateral negotiations, with my participation, and I was to head the multilateral
ones, with his. The importance of the bilateral negotiations derived from their perspective: they focused on the old views of each
side with the aim of settling any differences based on them. The
multilateral negotiations, in contrast, looked to the future, seeking
to establish a foundation for a new regional framework. Thus, the
bilateral talks concerned specific parties while the multilateral
ones addressed issues. In all, five working groups were set up to
cover each of the following categories: economics, water, refugees,
arms control, and ecology. Palestinian and Israeli delegations
would participate with delegations from an additional thirty countries, including the United States, Russia, representatives from the
European Community, China, Japan, India, and Canada. These
groups continue to meet biannually in different places, following
preparatory discussions.

The main drawback of the multilateral negotiations so far was that generally they had little long-term significance, and never had immediate significance. Everyone involved recognized that there was no chance of advancing along multilateral lines without the concomitant bilateral progress, and the bilateral talks showed few signs of real advancement. Thus, the multilateral negotiations looked like a promotional campaign for a glorious future, which would come about only if rescued from the bilateral morass.

I ran into snags as soon as I took office and became involved in the project. The European Community, which all along had wanted to help resolve the Middle East conflict, felt that it was being pushed out of the main—bilateral—arena, and was not given proper representation in the multilateral talks either. Israel suggested that the European role in the working groups be expanded, especially in the Committee for Arms Control, an area in which the Europeans showed much interest. We made an extra effort to explain the value of the multilateral talks, especially through personal contacts with Europe's top governmental and diplomatic people. The latter confirmed what I had long suspected: although it was true that without bilateral progress there would be no multilateral progress, the reverse was also true— there was no point in advancing along bilateral lines without an accompanying advance in the multilateral effort. In short, we had to work toward establishing a new Middle East based on prosperity and hope instead of poverty and anguish.

In my many conversations with European dignitaries during that first year of the Labor Alignment government, we outlined a program for a new Middle East following a European plan: economic cooperation first, followed by increasing, ongoing political understanding until stability was achieved. The idea ignited the imaginations of many of Israel's allies, including French President François Mitterrand, German Chancellor Helmut Kohl, and

Commissioner of the European Community Jacques Delors, who saw the grand possibilities of this new regional design for both Europe and the Middle East.

As a result, major European companies began to develop plans for expanding business in the Middle East. The World Bank swung into action, and the groundwork was laid for consolidating diverse activities. The Japanese offered to handle tourism, the French and Germans transportation and communications, the Italians the potential Red Sea–Dead Sea canal, the Austrians water and electricity, the British free trade, the Danes agriculture, the Americans human resources, and the Canadians refugees. Various steering committees were established to maintain contact among the working groups, especially between meetings. Even the two committees from which everyone expected nothing but heartache—Arms Control and Refugee Management—made some headway.

And it wasn't by chance.

In its very first meeting in Ottawa, on November 11–12, 1992, the Committee for Refugee Management ran into trouble. The Palestinians had appointed a member of the Palestine National Council as head of their team, in violation of the procedural rules set at the Madrid Conference. The crisis was settled only when I phoned the Egyptian Foreign Minister, Ahmru Mussah, who in turn approached the PLO leadership regarding the matter. PLO financier Abu Alaa received word of it and forced the resignation of the controversial head of the team. Despite its happy ending, the incident made it clear that the problems we would encounter would be as large as the attention paid to the multilateral negotiations was small.

The Palestinian delegations to the bilateral and the multilateral talks received instructions from PLO-appointed representatives.

For talks in Washington, it was Nabil Shath, a PLO spokesman whose image was familiar to television viewers the world over. For talks in Oslo, it was Abu Alaa, who submitted an economic development plan for the Middle East that I read with great interest. Although I could not agree with all of it, neither could I ignore the tremendous amount of work involved in its creation. I liked its originality and, especially, its constructive approach. Most Palestinian leaders—and many Israeli ones as well—live and breathe politics. They are interested only in the political issues and see economic matters as a bitter pill to swallow. Since most of the issues involved in the multinational negotiations were economic, it was natural that the PLO appoint Abu Alaa as its behind-the-scenes expert.

Abu Alaa's assistants helped our unofficial representatives in Oslo during the multilateral talks, and also during the more sensitive and complex bilateral talks. During my years as a public servant I have learned never to ignore suggestions from as-yet-unknown individuals, for the day may arrive when they become prominent.

At the same time, Israel tightened its relationship with Egypt. Egyptian Foreign Minister Mussah was keen on advancing the talks. Egypt was the only friendly face in the Arab world, not only for Israel but for the Palestinians as well. Syria had turned its back on the Palestinians, and, as I have said, Saudi Arabia refused to hear of Yasser Arafat. With Jordan, they had a friendly relationship on the surface, but suspicions raged internally. Egypt was a suitable way station in the Middle East for the United States, also. So, while the Oslo process picked up speed, Egypt worked behind the scenes to convince other Arabs of the sense of these ideas for a peaceful future. True, there was a need to reach a declaration of principles, but there was a need also to assign responsibility for

governing Gaza and Jericho. Then the PLO would have something to lean on, a place to call home.

To everyone's amazement—and even though the Americans
weren't involved—the multilateral negotiations began as sched-
uled. Here at last we had a venue far from the microphones and
cameras of Washington, D.C.—a communications channel that
would enable negotiations to take place discreetly and allow us,
finally, to get down to details. Of course, the dialogue began
slowly, step-by-step. It seemed strange at first, almost impossible
to achieve our goals, but as time passed we could discern for the
first time some small signs of flexibility among the Palestinians. It
was very encouraging, since when all is said and done, people
must be judged, not on hearsay, but on their deeds.

The setting was ideal. In Norway, no one was looking for
scoops. Even on my last trip to Oslo, not one newspaper reporter
requested to accompany me. *Déjà vu* was the general opinion
among the government-run communications authorities in Israel.
Why send a team to cover the visit? What could happen there?
Yet because the Oslo negotiations, unlike those in Washington,
were far from the eyes and ears of the media, we were able to keep
the talks going for months. The two sides could talk directly,
person-to-person, rather than simply spout rhetoric.

Norway is a magnificent country—beautiful scenery, extraor-
dinary people. A close-knit group of top government people
made itself available for passing messages between ourselves and
the PLO. The group included Foreign Minister Johann Jurgen
Holst and his wife, Marianne, and the head of the Political Research Institute, Terry Larsen, and his wife, Mona. They acted
with absolute discretion. When discussions began to intensify,
they spared no logistical or other effort to keep the momentum
going and to shield us from the curious. And as soon as I knew
the negotiations were to be taken seriously, I gave the Prime Min-

ister the background information and then kept him informed of every detail. Together, we worked out the directives to the Israeli delegation.

AT the time of the negotiations, I was preoccupied with some soul searching. I have always tended to be overly optimistic, while I also tow around a collection of old-fashioned ideas—the residues of earlier missions. I know that what happened to the Jews was unprecedented: a nation returned to its homeland and its ancient language after centuries. I thought that something unprecedented could also happen to the Palestinians: a group who had never been a people could now be a people among peoples.

It was clear to me that at the heart of this wearying, hundred-year-old conflict—a conflict exacerbated by the establishment of the State of Israel forty-five years ago—stood the Palestinian issue. After all, we did not enter into war with Egypt to take over half of Sinai; we did not clash with Syria to obtain the Golan Heights. For many years we had lived in peace with Lebanon, and never imagined fighting a war with that country. We did not go to war with Jordan to unite Jerusalem, which, like Berlin, was "a city and at its heart, a wall," to quote poet Noami Shemer. We were forced to enter these wars to save our lives; had we lost even one of them, we would have lost everything. Israel did not initiate the military hostilities. Egypt, Syria, Lebanon, and Jordan—and even Iraq, which has no common border with Israel—declared war on us because of the Palestinian issue. These were the only real grounds for our terrible wars.

It was not only war that took a toll. Victory itself opened a Pandora's box. We were forced to cope with unrelenting Arab hostilities, and to enforce law and order in territories settled mostly by embittered Arabs. It is easier to respond to a direct attack from an enemy than to deal with the gnawing opposition of a people who have lost their land but not their honor.

In addition, our collective conscience troubled us: we were in conflict with ourselves, not only with our neighbors. Throughout history, the Jewish people have recoiled from ruling others. Our forefathers never had colonial aspirations or missionary tendencies, nor do Israelis today. And, on a more personal note, our failure in London in 1987 continued to prey upon me. We could have saved ourselves and the Palestinians six years of *intifada,* and the loss of so much human life, had the former head of the Likud-run government not undermined the agreement I had worked out with King Hussein of Jordan.

There was no point in waiting any longer. The Likud government had run its course, and the political freeze—the product of its ideological beliefs—was over. Terrorism continued, and the demographics were changing fast. If Israel was not careful, it would lose its lead in population growth between the sea and the Jordan River, and thereby invite tragedy—the same sort of ethnic conflict that destabilized Yugoslavia. Yet as I carefully followed the bilateral negotiations in Washington, my doubts grew. I was terrified that the paper boats sailing in that sea of words would, one by one, crash against the rocks of the controversy called Jerusalem, or run aground on the sandbar called the settlements.

I T wasn't difficult for me to understand the decision-making process from the Palestinian side as well. It was increasingly apparent that the bottom line was Yasser Arafat. Although even those closest to him did not spare him their biting criticism, one fact hit home: Yasser Arafat had no replacement. He had succeeded in attaining a position that is difficult to reach and even more difficult to ignore. Arafat is, in effect, a national symbol, a legend in his own time, a myth in the eyes of the Palestinians. And where myth begins, arguments end. Even though I completely rejected his strategy, I did not underestimate his tactical talents. Arafat knew that there is no substitute for negotiation. He would not allow his delegates to retreat from the talks; each time they showed signs of hesitation, he sent them back to the table. He also understood, however, that any agreement reached without him would undermine his power and the organization he headed. So each time his delegation got uncomfortably close to any agreement with Israel, Arafat halted the progress.

In his twenty-five years of leadership, Arafat has shown both personal courage and manipulative skills. It is not by pure luck that he has managed to survive for so long. Arafat began serving as head of the PLO during Lyndon Johnson's tenure as President of the United States, and managed to keep his job with the Nixon, Ford, Carter, Reagan, Bush, and Clinton administrations in power. With regard to Israel, he has stuck it out through Eshkol, Meir, Rabin, Begin, Shamir, Peres, Shamir again, and Rabin again. For a quarter of a century he has been leading a national coalition without nationhood, maintaining elections without being elected. A coalition that does not have a country to run generally keeps busy by formulating and publishing declarations. But a declaration is not a country. You can expand or cut it. You can add a sentence or change an expression or revise a paragraph, and the coalition will continue to exist. Napoleon said that he would rather fight against a coalition than as a part of it.

Arafat used the declaration of principles to gain the upper hand in his power struggle with his adversaries within the coalition. Until he heard an offer that he was unable to refuse, he preferred to continue with things as they were rather than risk angering his people with a clear decision or endangering the internal structure of his organization. To ensure that the Palestinian delegation not veer from his stand, he instructed them to hold fast on the inclusion of East Jerusalem in any autonomy settlement.

The delegation did as he asked, and the negotiations were deadlocked.

I KNEW that if we did not make direct contact with Yasser Arafat, the negotiations would remain at a standstill. But to do so was anathema to Israeli citizens, whom we represented. It also ran counter to government decisions and the 1975 agreement we had made with the United States. Moreover, recognition of Arafat harbored additional dangers. What if we recognize him, but he does not change his stand? The very fact of our recognition, together with that of the United States, would give him gratis what he had been seeking all along. An evermore confident Arafat might dig in his heels, and we would have to negotiate in some no-man's-land between the territories and Tunis, between the interim agreement and the Palestinian state.

Oddly enough, it was thanks to this very predicament that the opportunity arose to conduct a dialogue with Arafat. In the midst of the controversy, we could try to agree on the contents of negotiation before we agreed on mutual recognition. In other words, we would negotiate with Arafat without acknowledging his authority. Absolute secrecy was a necessity, and the Norwegians were a gift from heaven.

One day my friend, author Amos Oz, called me. "Shimon," he asked, "did you ever think about what would happen should the PLO cave in completely?" Indeed, I felt that the PLO was losing ground. For years, most people believed that relations between Israel and the PLO were at zero sum, whereby the advantages of one side automatically become the disadvantages of the other. Would a PLO collapse benefit Israel? If the great enemy against whom we had been fighting these many years suddenly disappeared, who would take its place? Was Hamas a preferable alternative? Should we negotiate with these fundamentalists? After all, Hamas is under the thumb of Iran, and Iran sees Israel as the collective reflection of Salman Rushdie. The Iran of today—extremist to the point of insanity—wants to destroy Israel and the peace process. How can we come to an agreement on bilateral recognition when Hamas denies our very existence?

Thus, circumstances at the time in the region and in the territories led us to conclude that perhaps it was in Israel's interest to have the PLO play a role on this political stage. And there were parallel signs of change within the PLO. Its members could no longer rely solely on their pact calling for the destruction of Israel, and they were no longer so sure of themselves or of their ability to use terror to achieve international aims. The dynamics of the negotiations had made them rethink the utility of terror. I knew that we could not push the PLO to the breaking point. Just as Israel could not carry a burden it could not lift, we could not load the PLO with an impossibly heavy burden. They too had problems, and they too had to find a happy medium between their goals and their ability to achieve them.

I REVIEWED the Alon plan, developed in 1967, which proposed giving up most of the West Bank, excluding the Jordan valley in the east; and Moshe Dayan's 1967 plan to relinquish most of the West Bank, excluding the western edge between the Israeli border and the Golan Heights. Neither proposal was practical. The Likud government had established settlements in the West Bank, and now approximately 120,000 Israelis lived there. It would be unthinkable to force them to leave, unless we wanted to risk a civil war.

The Likud government did not annex Judea and Samaria, despite its historical significance, initially because of coalition agreements with Moshe Dayan and with Yigal Yadin's party, and later because of obligations under the Camp David agreement, which eliminated the possibility of annexation. Nevertheless, they complicated the chances of a solution because of outdated concepts based on obsolete strategic and historical arguments. Preventing an Arab military incursion from the east could, indeed, be realistic, under certain circumstances, but not when weighed against two other, more imminent dangers: internal terrorist activity, which was expected to increase along with an increase in the Arab population; and missile attacks, which make irrelevant the 30 to 50 kilometer "strategic depth" that Israel gives as a reason for holding on to the entire West Bank, not to mention the Gaza Strip, which has negligible benefit to national security nowadays. As for the historical perspective, one of the great Jewish thinkers, Professor Yehezkiel Kaufman, wrote: "There is no connection between secure boundaries and the true land of Israel; nor between them and the area of the State of Israel from time immemorial; nor between them and the ideal land or the ideal state to which the nation aspired in historic times."[1]

I came up with the idea of "Gaza first" in 1980. I thought it would make things easier if we could reach an agreement in two strokes—first Gaza, then the West Bank. I preferred Gaza first because, unlike Jerusalem (I was convinced we would make no compromise there), it was not emotionally or politically sensitive, and unlike the West Bank, it was not peppered with Israeli settlements.

The Gaza Strip is more than a territory; it is a population. Roughly 800,000 people live in an area covering only 365 square kilometers (140 square miles). Within this narrow area, the Israeli army controls some parts for purposes of security and public order, while other parts are controlled by settlers. The Palestinians in Gaza have an extremely low standard of living, and their income depends on their link with Israel. Many residents are war refugees who live in camps with very poor health and housing conditions. The city of Gaza is 7,000 years old—7,000 years of suffering. Israel has no resources either to rehabilitate the Gaza Strip or to improve the plight of its people. Nor can we come to terms with a severe refugee problem in the area under our control. What good is control if we cannot improve conditions? What is Israel's moral mandate? What are our political grounds? Samson, in his time, took a drastic step, bringing down the columns of the shrine in Gaza. There was no point in our repeating it.

I also viewed it as a mistake to attempt to suppress the violence of a minority of radical Palestinians in Gaza, while at the same time guarding the lives of the unarmed, peaceful majority. In the end, of course, the law-abiding citizens of Gaza were forced to pay the price for the terrorist activities of a few. In response to stabbings of Israeli employers and innocent bystanders, we were forced to close the border with Gaza. There was no historical sense in our policing Gaza, when every Israeli soldier who defended himself against a knife-wielding or rock-throwing Palestinian was blamed in the world press for violating human rights. It was a hopeless task and no good could come of it. The Palestinians would have to run their own lives, elect their own leaders, and hold weapons legally for their self-defense.

Not one Arab country has shown a readiness to annex the Gaza Strip. Yasser Arafat well understood the situation and turned his attention to Gaza, where he could gain not only yet another television appearance but also a territorial foothold. Israel too, I believe, had an interest in his doing so. A two-pronged

Palestinian leadership—one in Tunis and one in the territories—
would not be able to control Gaza because of its split political
personality and the dual loyalty of activists in the area. The only
way to rid ourselves of the impossible burden of the Gaza Strip
was to allow a centralized PLO leadership to settle there and cope
with its problems directly.

But, again, how could this be accomplished? I assumed if we
proposed "Gaza first," the Palestinians would suspect we were
offering "Gaza only." Without a clear sign for continued negotiations regarding the West Bank, the Palestinians could not agree. I
had also learned that offers made out of hand tend to be rejected,
whereas those made in response to a demand are considered victories. In other words, the chance of getting "Gaza first" depended on two prerequisites: that it be "Gaza plus" and that the
Palestinians ask for it.

If in Oslo we discovered the way to meet with the PLO leadership, in Egypt we found the spark to ignite the talks, maintain the
energy, and find a creative solution. I traveled to Egypt twice
during the critical period between November 15, 1992 and July
5–6 1993. President Hosni Mubarak, Foreign Minister Ahmru
Mussah, and Adviser Osmah el-Baaz were privy to the fact that
secret talks were under way. President Mubarak, whose effort to
advance the peace process has not received sufficient recognition,
showed great willingness to assist both sides. We held long, honest
discussions in which I described to the Egyptian statesmen the
Israeli limitations and the Palestinian possibilities. Foreign Minister Mussah maintained contact with both sides, and every time we
reached a dead end, I would call him and he would take action.
Osmah el-Baaz, sharp as a razor, did not for one minute lose faith
that we would reach a settlement. Finally the offer was framed
and consolidated, with Gaza and Jericho first in accordance with
demands by the PLO.

I was satisfied. That was exactly what was needed.

I preferred to offer Jericho as a sign of our intent to continue negotiations, even if "Gaza first" would be the main policy. There were no Jewish settlements in the immediate Jericho area, therefore there would be no need to discuss their fate. We proposed that an administrative center be set up in Jericho to take the pressure off Jerusalem, especially since Jericho is not far from Jerusalem. Its proximity to the Jordan River opened a preferred solution, in my eyes, for the future: a confederation between the Jordanians and the Palestinians, something they would both need to prevent a future clash. Both sides had declared their readiness to accept such an arrangement as the basis for a permanent solution, even if it fell short of original expectations.

Slowly, the head of the Palestinian delegation came round, and after a difficult labor, an agreement was born, while a second was already in utero. Oddly enough, the agreement we reached dealt with the infamous declaration of principles. But in contrast to the Washington negotiations, the Oslo accord also included a paragraph on the Gaza Strip and Jericho. Thus, in Oslo the Palestinians gained not only philosophical principles, though important in themselves, but also land. Israel offered to sign immediately on all points affirmed and to put off to a later date discussion of those issues not yet affirmed. The presence of the PLO in Gaza would prove—to themselves and to their public—their ability to control specific situations, maintain law and order, and prevent Hamas from wreaking havoc.

The accord had to stand by itself, independent of agreements with other parties to the Madrid Conference. After being initialed in Oslo, the agreement would be subject to approval by the relevant bodies: the government of Israel and "Palestinian representatives" (not specifically defined). The official ratification ceremony would be held in Washington.

THE negotiations in Oslo and in Egypt lasted approximately eight months, until the morning of August 18, 1993. They hit the usual high and low points. There were times when one side or the other almost gave up. And then one day I was able to cable Norwegian Foreign Minister Johann Holst: "The positions have been clarified. Trust has been generated. The limitations have been tested. The time has come for an accord."

As I wrote those lines, there lay before me a letter brought by my good friend, newspaper reporter Mira Avrech, from a most unexpected source, a man I did not know. Bassam Abu Sharif, personal aide to Yasser Arafat, had written me a heartwarming letter on June 23—that is, six weeks before my note to Holst. There are only few times in history, I thought, that a man in his situation could write such things to a man in my situation.

I held in my hand the official stationery of the office of Yasser Arafat, under the heading: "The State of Palestine—The Organization for the Freedom of Palestine—Office of the President." I read his words over and over. They were handwritten, in English. I read, and I knew: we were almost home free.

June 23rd, 1993

His Excellency Mr. Shimon Peres
The Minister of Foreign Affairs of the State of Israel

Dear Mr. Peres,

It is, indeed, an exciting opportunity for me to be able to write you a letter and be sure that it will be delivered to you personally. I decided to send it handwritten, rather than typed, because I thought this will give you an indication as to the feelings I have towards a peaceful future and life we are struggling for.

Dear Mr. Peres, I am sure that Israelis want peace, the same way Palestinians want it. Extremists on both sides will ebb the moment men of courage and caliber step forward to bridge the gap and to break the barrier of fear and distrust. Both Israelis and Palestinians have an opportunity now to do it. Both Israelis and Palestinians need *men* on the top to start it.

It will not be a pity only if we miss the opportunity, it will be unfortunate and catastrophic for all of us. That is why we are working hard, day and night, to push the process forward. But let me be very frank with you. Palestinians find it impossible (practically) to achieve progress if the direct contacts between the Israeli government and the PLO leadership remain "non-grata." A breakthrough is needed. One that can create a new momentum.

I believe that an arrangement for a top-level meeting is possible under the present international and Arab conditions. That will definitely create a positive chain reaction that will help to break the ice rapidly.

We admire in you, your clear vision to the future, your ability to grasp the new in this world, and your genuine ideas that aim at the creation of a new Middle East. That we share with you.

When we examine deeply the positions of the Israeli ministers, you spring among them as the one who has enough of a historical figure to be able to start a better future.

We hope that you do invest all the fine qualities that you

do possess, in the process of creating the better future. We are ready to do that, to put our hands in yours to build a stable and flourishing future for your and our future generations.

Ready to respond for any initiative in that direction, I remain dedicated to the cause of peace between the Arabs and Israelis.

Sincerely,

Bassam Abu Sharif

AT home, things were not so simple. The Prime Minister and I ensured that no details of our many private conversations were leaked to the press, so that we were free to discuss each issue on its own merits, without worrying about public relations or internal politics. Likewise, Yitzhak Rabin had acted wisely in closing off the territories to maintain the personal security of Israeli citizens. Needless to say, we had no intention of endangering our achievement by taking an incautious step. However, in addition to security considerations, we faced a difficult coalition problem.

Of the 120 members of Knesset, 67 supported the government. Of these, 5 represented Arab parties. One of the other parties—Shas—was already threatening to quit the coalition for reasons not even remotely connected with the peace process. Sure enough, on the night when the accord was signed, 6 Shas members pulled out, and we remained with a majority of only 61 votes. True, in a democracy, a majority of one is still a majority, but it is difficult to build a new national agreement on such a shaky foundation, especially considering that this majority hinged on the votes of our Arab members.

But these political considerations had given the negotiations an added push. There is a limit to the weight so narrow a majority could carry. On all four fronts, Israel was being asked to make the majority of the concessions: Syria wanted the Golan Heights; Lebanon wanted the Israel Defense Forces (IDF) to pull out of the security zone; Jordan demanded that the border be changed in its favor; and Palestinians wanted Judea, Samaria, and Gaza. We had understood that we must not stop the talks with any of them. However, it was also necessary to clarify the prospects of overall peace in the Middle East, not merely peace between any two of its parties. We had agreed to speed the pace of talks in each sector, depending on the circumstances. At the time, the chances of success with the Palestinians weren't particularly promising, and the Syrian situation looked like a Gordian knot that no one was in any hurry to cut.

The Palestinian delegation had pushed hard for autonomy in Jerusalem as well, and had demanded that all new Israeli settlements in the territories be stopped. According to the Palestinian view, even building in Jerusalem was considered "settlement." Then on July 29, 1993, I appeared with Faisal Husseini in a joint interview on Israeli television. This was the first time a minister of the Israeli government appeared in a public broadcast with a Palestinian leader. I explained that our stand was unequivocal: just as we do not demand that the Arabs stop building in Jerusalem, so also they cannot demand that we do so. Palestinian residents of Jerusalem would be allowed to vote in the autonomy elections, but they could not be elected to its institutions because the autonomy accord would not apply to Jerusalem. Moreover, Israel made it clear that it had no intention of destroying existing Jewish settlements in the territories. Just as Arab settlements could live under a rule that was not Arab, so also Jewish settlements could live under a rule that was not Israeli.

Mr. Rabin, who had dual responsibility as Prime Minister and as Defense Minister, was worried about the security issue, right-fully so. Without a secure future, there was no point to an agreement; and in any case, Israel would not accept it. When we discussed this subject between ourselves, those waiting outside joked about the six-way ministerial meeting, including two prime ministers (one currently in power), two ministers of defense (one currently in power), one foreign minister, and one former chief of staff.

IN Oslo, Israel achieved more than just words. We got concessions without which we would never have been able to sign an agreement. These include responsibility for security against threats from outside our borders and responsibility for the security of every Israeli in the territories. Jerusalem remains outside the autonomy accord, although its Palestinian residents will be able to participate in elections for autonomy. The settlements stay where they are, and settlement security stays in the capable hands of the IDF. We promised to continue negotiations on autonomy for other areas within Judea and Samaria after the elections, which were targeted for nine months from October 13, 1993, the day the declaration of principles went into effect. Until then, Israel would transfer five important areas of administration—health, education, welfare, tourism, and taxes—to the Palestinians.

WHEN we signed the first agreement with the PLO, the second was already under way. The latter was intended to end the deep conflict between the two sides and set the stage for general, official, and public talks. The PLO had tremendous interest in this, for all the time it remained unrecognized by Israel, it was as the poet Uri Zvi Greenberg put it, "grass on the side of the road."

Israel had specific conditions regarding its recognition by the
PLO: that the PLO publicly acknowledge the right of Israel to
exist within secure borders and in peace; that the PLO accept
United Nations' Security Council resolutions 242 and 338 as the
foundation for negotiation; that the PLO cease using terrorism
and instead fight against terror and terrorism; that the PLO be
obligated to settle future differences by political negotiation instead of with the use of violence; and—mainly—that the PLO
nullify the thirty-three articles of the Palestinian Covenant, which
call for, directly (twenty-eight) or by implication (five), the destruction of Israel. We requested a fundamental change in PLO
principles in accordance with the revised version of the pact and
the deletion of its antipeace statements.

Israel had notified all parties involved that, should we reach an
agreement, we would recognize the PLO as the representative of
the Palestinian people, after we coordinated arrangements with
the United States. I kept in mind the wise advice of Winston
Churchill: it is better to jump across an abyss with one step rather
than with two. A mutual recognition between Israel and the PLO
might be more meaningful than the declaration of principles. An
outright recognition could become possible if and when the PLO
changes its basic policy toward Israel.

Once this matter was settled, Foreign Minister Holst and I
flew to California, where U.S. Secretary of State Warren Christopher was vacationing. In honor of the occasion, he interrupted his
holiday to meet us, in the company of Dennis Ross, coordinator of
the State Department's "peace group." I opened by apologizing
to Mr. Christopher for interfering with his holiday and thanked
him for his time.

"This," said Christopher, "is the sort of event it's worth inter-
rupting for."

"There are two ways in which to end the conflict with the

PLO," I continued. "With the power of power or with the power of wisdom. Wisdom is better than power. If we all act wisely, the PLO will become a partner in peace instead of an obstacle to it."

Holst reminded Christopher of the general reports he had submitted to him on our meetings in Oslo, and the Secretary thanked him for them. He began to read the agreement, studying it with the scrutiny of an experienced attorney and the eye of a politician. He noted briefly: "It seems to me you have done a fabulous job, touching on every aspect of a wide range of topics. My first reaction is very positive." With the nod of approval from our friends the Americans, we could fly home and report that all systems were go.

IN our conversations with the Palestinians, they often stressed a strong desire for financial assistance. We too had an interest in helping them, because he who lives in comfort promises comfort also to his neighbor. I have always believed that political victories not accompanied by economic benefit stand on very shaky ground. You can celebrate victory with bullhorns, but bullhorns won't put breakfast on the table.

Therefore, I shuttled back and forth among the countries involved to show them the economic side of the Middle East peace achievement. The Scandinavian countries have always been sensitive to the distress and suffering of other nations, and regularly donate 1 to 2 percent of their GNP to those in need. I asked them in the name of Israel to target 5 percent of their foreign aid to help the Palestinians establish an independent government. They were extremely generous and immediately agreed.

Then I met the head of the European Community, Jacques Delors, along with Hans van den Broek, the former Minister of

Foreign Affairs of the Netherlands, and Delors's team. I found him enthusiastic about extending immediate aid. But he was also prepared to do more, hoping to get the European Community to help build a sound economic infrastructure on the level of Europe's. I had a long conversation with French President Mitterrand in his lovely retreat in the midst of a wonderful forest in the Pyrenees. Thereafter, I spoke with most of Europe's foreign ministers. All were eager to extend a hand.

At the same time, we ironed out the final wrinkles on mutual recognition with the PLO. Holst hurried to Tunis to get Arafat's signature on the declaration of recognition of Israel, and then came to Jerusalem so Prime Minister Rabin could sign the declaration of recognition of the PLO.

Everything was ready. On September 12, we left for Washington: Prime Minister Rabin, Minister of Science and Communications Shulamit Aloni, and I, together with a group of assistants and families of fallen soldiers—the true heroes of the Middle East tragedy and without whom Israel would not have reached this breakthrough.

Even at the eleventh hour, we met with serious difficulties. On September 13, shortly before the ceremony on the White House lawn was to begin, Dr. Ahmed Tibi, an adviser of Yasser Arafat, appeared at my hotel room to inform me that, if we did not consent to certain changes in a number of sentences in the declaration, Arafat would be on the next plane home. Among other items, the Palestinians wanted to delete the paragraph in which their group is mentioned as a part of the "Jordanian-Palestinian delegation" and to initial "PLO" at each point where the expression "the Palestinian team" was mentioned. After conferring with Rabin, I answered in the negative to the first demand and positively to the second. Since we had recognized the PLO, there was no reason why its name could not be noted. But Arafat was not satisfied and notified us, via Tibi, that he was leaving.

"If so," I told Tibi, "I have one request of you. Let me know when you're going, because we will be going, too."

The PLO representative then asked that the term *PLO* be typed in, not remain as a penciled correction. I agreed to that immediately, and the crisis was diffused. The fate of a far-reaching historical transition had hinged on the difference between the lead of a pencil and the ribbon of a printer.

ON the White House lawn, President Clinton orchestrated the handshake between Prime Minister Rabin and Chairman Arafat and the ceremonial ratification of the agreement. Only after I had signed in the name of Israel did I see rows of emotional faces before me. Many people came over to congratulate me, describing the event as one of the most important and most moving of the twentieth century. They felt this way because, for so many years, it had seemed that the Palestinian-Israeli rift was unbridgeable. Nevertheless, we had discovered the right formulation, a sign that it could be found again in later, bloodless, disputes.

I was almost more thoughtful than I was happy. I had already gone beyond this ceremony to the next step: how to build a new Middle East. Resolving past differences was not enough. We also had to look forward, to construct a framework that held a potential for happiness for all peoples in the region. This was not the time for memories. It was a time to form a new agenda. The accord in Oslo and the ceremony in Washington were but a stepping-stone from which to leap, higher and farther than ever before.

2

AT THE
CROSSROADS

MANY OF MY FRIENDS, AND EVEN MORE OF
my opponents, have asked me how my concern for the armed
defense of Israel (for almost twenty years I served in various secu-
rity-related positions, including Director-General of the Ministry
of Defense and Deputy Minister of Defense, as well as Prime
Minister) has been supplanted by fervent dedication to the peace
process. I see no reason to apologize, but I will explain. As far as I
can tell, it was not I who shifted course from the traditional concept of national defense, which depends mainly on military and
weapons systems, to the modern concept, which is of necessity
based on political accords, and embraces international security

and economic considerations. Rather, the world has changed. And
the process of change compels us to replace our outdated concepts with an approach tailored to the new reality.

The traditional school of defense has no answer to today's
geographical reality or technological threat. The geographical issue arose with the development of long-range ballistic missiles.
Now, the physical considerations of the traditional strategy—natural obstacles, man-made structures, troop mobilizations, location
of the battlefields—are irrelevant in a defense against missile attacks. Even the targeted defense weaponry—the antimissile missiles—are almost useless and require exorbitant financial outlays.
The significance of the term "strategic depth" has been reduced,
with the ballistics criterion replacing the geographic one.

But there's more. There is absolutely no military answer to
unconventional weaponry, which does not distinguish the rear
from the front and which bestows a new—and terrible—meaning
to the term "total war." Thanks to long-range missiles, these unconventional instruments of destruction can reach directly into
populated areas, and people are helpless against the tremendous
damage they wreak.

There is, however, an alternative approach: bilateral and multilateral pacts, extending beyond the borders of the countries involved and covering the entire expanse within reach of the deadly
missiles—that is, treaties that cover whole regions. The countries
in a region must cooperate to counteract the nuclear, biological,
and chemical menace by creating a state of affairs that makes
conflicts too costly, too impractical, and too difficult. Thus, the
key to maintaining an equable and safe regional system is in politics and in economics. Today, maintaining a high standard of living requires competitive trade relations, open borders, and
reliance on science and technology. True power—even military

power—is no longer anchored in the boot camp, but on the university campuses. Politics should pave the way from pure military strategy to an enriched political and economic repertoire.

IN the past, national relations were contingent on quantitative factors: size of an area, natural resources, population density, location. Countries competed to own or control these resources. This rivalry sired hostility, which was often quickly translated into a clash of arms. The victor won real, physical assets, and believed it had obtained its goal. In truth, however, it had only opened the next round in a vicious cycle, as the new status demanded that old strategies be adapted to new conditions.

Toward the end of the twentieth century, relations between nations began to take on a new, qualitative dimension. There was increasing significance in scientific progress, rapid communications, methods of data collection, higher education, artificial intelligence, high technology, and fostering a peaceful environment that creates wealth and goodwill. These are the elements of contemporary power. The scale has tipped in the direction of economics rather than military might. Armies might conquer physical entities, but they cannot conquer qualitative ones. At this stage of the game, objects that may be subject to a military takeover are no longer of value.

In addition, we dare not forget the ever-growing difficulty of maintaining a huge army—regrettably, still an inescapable fact of life in the Middle East—to neutralize potential enemies in the absence of peace. The costs of weapons systems and military hardware have gone through the ceiling; it now hinders a country's national ability to cope with other, truly important challenges. After all, we already know that per-acre productivity is more important than the size of the farm, advanced technology is more important than the extent of natural reserves, and broad-based knowledge is more important than population size.

What is right for the rest of the world is right for Israel and the Arab nations as well. Fate has brought us from a world of territorial conflict to one of economic challenge and of new opportunities created by human intellectual advances. History, as Professor Paul Kennedy once wrote, creates a new winners and losers list.[1] The Middle East is now a winner. The ball is in our court.

THE Middle East is the storehouse of humankind's collective memories as much as it is a quagmire of regional conflict. The first stones of Western civilization were laid here, and it was from here that the spark of monotheism illuminated the world, destroying the dominion of pagan deities. Moses and Hammurabi laid down the fundamentals of lawful government here, carved on tablets, for all to know and heed. The prophets of Israel preached here, followed by the founders of the other great monotheistic religions, Jesus and Muhammad, who spread their doctrines of peace, justice, and morality for all. And it was here, in the expanse of the Fertile Crescent, the Syro-African Rift, and on the banks of the Nile, that people began to harness nature for their own needs, controlling the power of the great rivers to reap harvests from the barren land. The Nile Delta, the valley of the Tigris and Euphrates, the Sinai Desert, and the Judean Hills all nurtured the burgeoning civilization we are part of today. And here it also encountered the culture of reason and beauty that was classical Greece.

And the rest is history.

Since antiquity the Middle East has played a key role in the welfare of all people. This region was essential to the security of world trade routes and to the stability of the great empires that rose and fell, their rulers always paying attention to happenings here. There was no period in which the Middle East did not ignite the imagination of prophets and dreamers, travelers and explorers, traders and adventurers, fighters and rulers—and especially, followers of the three great monotheistic religions, believers in divine revelation. After all, it was from here that the Lord's agents spread the word of the Almighty. Here too, people were mesmerized by the area; beyond the sizzling white desert sands, along the hazy horizon, they could discern the long-lost Garden of Eden. Thus, the Middle East served not only as a center of trade and travel but as the focal point of people's spiritual life—their path to the gateway of heaven. It is no wonder, then, that foreign interests and expectations have influenced the history of the Middle East more than that of any other area of the world. The ancient Greeks and Romans; the medieval Crusaders; and contemporary French, English, Russian, and U.S. leaders all, at one point or another, have focused their attention on the Middle East, have became involved in its events, have seized its strategic posts, and have attempted to affect its development.

With decolonization in the second half of the twentieth century, Western involvement in Middle Eastern events, and jockeying for control of the area, increased hand-in-hand with the Middle East's growing involvement in Western planning and economics. The energy crisis of the 1970s and its manipulation by certain oil-producing Arab countries against the background of the Yom Kippur War brought this process to a head. However, the distress and pain of Westerners who stood in line for hours to buy gas and who froze through the bleak winter of 1974 did not solve the problems of the Middle Eastern countries. Spurred in great part by the Arab-Israeli conflict, the arms race continued with a vengeance. The bulk of the area's resources were diverted to the construction of a military infrastructure, to an extent far exceeding the economic and social capabilities of the countries involved. The entire region stagnated; its tremendous developmental potential was left by the wayside, the well-being of its inhabitants neglected.

Prolongation of the Arab-Israeli conflict has inevitably led to the continued misery of millions. In frustration, many of these people have turned to mysticism and otherworldliness, have rejected the modernist state, and have immersed themselves in religious fundamentalism. These are the factors that now threaten the stability and peace of the area and jeopardize global interests. Over 1 billion Muslims worldwide look to the Middle East as the source of life and a wellspring of belief. In Central Asia and the Far East, in Africa, Europe, and America, Muslims face Mecca when kneeling in prayer, while thousands make the pilgrimage there each year. Mecca, Medina, and Jerusalem; Cairo, Damascus, and Baghdad—these are the centers of Islamic inspiration, values, and culture.

The history of Western civilization cannot be fully understood without considering the contributions Islamic culture has made to contemporary science, philosophy, mathematics, literature, art, and trade. Today we are witnessing a renaissance of Islamism, now characterized by opposition to Western values and culture, a retreat from modernism, and a call for the use of force to establish an autocratic, suppressive Islamic republic. In a fervent national revolution, one radical Muslim sect—the Shia—installed the Ayatollah Khomeini in Iran. Members of another sect, the Sunni, orchestrated the murder of Egyptian President Anwar el-Sadat and currently threaten not only the strongest Arab nation but also the stability of the absolutist government in Saudi Arabia, the more moderate one of King Hussein in Jordan, and even the presidency of Hafiz al-Assad in Syria. Among Palestinians, Islamic extremists are fighting for control and influence, and not only on a spiritual level or in the mosques. All fundamentalist manifestos have a dual common denominator. They express societal distress, formulated in religious-moralist terms; at the same time, they express the distress of the believers—Muslim devotees who feel that they are in the midst of a struggle for survival under conditions of modernism and permissiveness, which pose a threat to simple, innocent piety.[2]

It may be said that the process of modernization shifts the promise of the Garden of Eden in the next world to its realization in this one. To the Muslim fundamentalist, the greater the distress in this world, the higher the expectations of a better life in the world to come. And the path to that afterlife is religious fundamentalist revolution. Therefore, the present wave of fundamentalism engulfing many areas of the Middle East threatens the very stability of the social order. It is not derived from the conflict with Israel or from the embryonic peace process. Rather, its opposition to the existence of the State of Israel, which is perceived by them as a foreign body in the service of an oppressive and heretical, imperialist government, is part and parcel of its inherent resistance to modernism per se.

The classic symbol of Middle Eastern fundamentalism is the Ayatollah Khomeini. His government was founded on total rejection of the advances instituted by the Shah of Iran and mass hatred of Western culture and everything it stands for. But Khomeini did borrow one principle from two flawed and oppressive Western forms of government. Despite the fact that both communism and fascism are essentially secular and negate the existence of God and the word of Muhammad, they demand absolute obedience of the citizenry and punish unmercifully those who stray. Khomeini adopted this dictatorial rule, not in the name of a secular ideology but in the "name of Allah." By claiming to enforce the will of God, he assumed the right to suppress all those who opposed him. His theocracy was tailored to suit the perplexity of our times, to provide an answer for the muddled masses perturbed by the impotence of Westernized society and its failure to provide the promised economic and social prosperity. To an entire generation of pained and confused youth grappling with a complex and difficult world, Khomeini's solution seems simple and unambiguous: It supplies instant spiritual satisfaction and a clearly defined path to a happy afterlife. They need only follow the teachings of Islam, as interpreted by Khomeini. The key to salvation rests in the hands of each and every individual.

Professor Emmanuel Sivan's comparative study of the two important Muslim sects—the Shia, who follow Khomeini, and the Sunni, of the school of the Muslim Brotherhood—revealed that the message of the two movements is very similar:

Diagnosis. Islam today, in the twentieth century, is threatened by a danger . . . so great that it surpasses in scope and depth anything encountered before. This time the danger is from within, from Islamic personalities and movements. Although sincere in their concern for the good of their nation, they have willingly imbibed the "magic potion" of Western ideology (nationality, socialism, liberalism, economic development, democracy). These "intoxicated" Muslims . . . are Muslims in name only . . . and the result is that the Islamic world is in a state of heresy, all the more dangerous because it is invisible. *Remedy.* True believers must return to the political fold from which they have long been absent. They must systematically and severely criticize all aspects of modernism in Muslim disguise. . . . Radicals must not cringe from the inevitable conclusion: delegitimization of existing regimes. *Treatment.* After the preparatory stage, the delegitimization of such mighty regimes must necessarily lead to armed uprising and takeover of governmental control by the political vanguard of Islam.[3]

Is it any wonder then, that Khomeini's followers intend to spread the Islamic revolution? In the wake of the Shah and his reformist "Green Revolution," Khomeini sallied forth under the banner of a "heavenly revolution" of believers that would pose a real threat to worldly "rapprochement." "Khomeinism" is a conceptual product, inherent in and originating from the system itself; and as such, it is a threat to the peace and stability of the entire region. With the destruction of communism, there remains only Khomeinism as the sole proponent of the principle of the end justifying the means: to achieve its lofty revolutionary goal of establishing the kingdom of Allah and the holy Imams on earth, one may lie, bribe, steal, and murder. Fundamentalism guarantees terrorists a place in the Garden of Eden, and they are prepared to endanger their lives for a short time in this lowly, wretched world in exchange for a blessed eternal life in the next one. Their fervent devotion to their so-called missions and their preparedness to sacrifice themselves on the altar of belief are wielded to spread a perilous hope. And as we stand on the threshold of the twenty-first century, the ability of an important people to progress and improve is being stifled.

This threat has become more tangible recently with Iran's attainment of nuclear capability. Can we count on extremists who believe they hold the keys to the kingdom of heaven to act with restraint—which requires a measure of rationality—once they get hold of nuclear power?

And Iran, of course, is not the only one. It has been widely reported that Iraq has tried, and continues in its efforts, to acquire nuclear power. It has already used chemical weapons in the Iran-Iraq War and the suppression of Kurdish uprisings. So why is it that with each revelation of an attempt by Saddam Hussein to obtain nuclear weapons, the world expresses anew its surprise and shock? Even Libya's radical leader, Muammar Qaddafi, a bird of another feather, is trying his luck in this sensitive and very dangerous area.

The danger of nuclear weapons in the hands of religious fanatics cannot be exaggerated.[4] It poses a menace not only to their immediate neighbors and to the region but to the entire world. The deadly combination of religious fundamentalism, missiles, and unconventional weaponry threatens peace and brings home once again the fact that it's a small world, after all.

The persistent conflict in the Middle East adds another dimension to this danger. The protracted tragedy of Lebanon, the hopeless struggle of the Kurds, the civil war in Sudan, the war between Iran and Iraq in the 1980s and the continuing hegemonist struggle in the Persian Gulf, Saddam Hussein's ambitions and his power-hungry attempts to annex Kuwait, and finally, the Arab-Israeli conflict, all obscure the path to development and advancement. Instead of investing in building and developing the region, the arms race, military buildups, wars, destruction, and devastation bleed the region of its main resources.

Nevertheless, the most pernicious threat remains the spread of Khomeinism. Thanks to their huge oil industry, the Khomeini radicals have an annual income of $15 billion from oil alone at their disposal. In light of the present military status of Iraq, Iran today enjoys strategic superiority, and the Ayatollahs are busy fanning the flames in every country within reach, from Egypt and the Sudan to Turkey. Mostly, though, they are eyeing Saudi Arabia. The eastern, oil-rich part of the kingdom is bursting with Shiite extremists. Not much imagination is necessary to guess what they are up to while they wait for the right moment. As Muhammad Hussein Fedlallah, leader of the Lebanese Hizballah terrorist organization, put it: "Man must take the initiative, since Allah helps only those who help themselves."[5]

Like the Shiites, the Sunni extremists also consider the eradication of "sinful" political leaders a sacred deed, to be accomplished by any means. They believe that this command is more important than *jihad* against Israel. "Only after we complete the release of our country from the worship of the gods of Ba'ath, will we turn against Israel," declared Husseini Aabu, leader of the Syrian fundamentalist terror organization Bahlav, before his judges, after suppression of the revolt against President Assad.[6] Similarly, in his recent book, Abed Alsalaam Farouj, ideologue of the underground movement responsible for the murder of President Sadat, wrote: "The enemy is the present rulers. Our immediate duty is to fight these rulers. This is the true Islamic *jihad* today, the highest calling in whose name all Muslims must pour their sweat and spill their blood."[7] Thus, the endless pressure of the extremists in Egypt along with the recent electoral achievements obtained by their friends in Jordan and Algeria make the fundamentalist threat to the entire region very real indeed.

E V E N the periphery is no longer safe. The breakup of the Soviet Union has made the newly independent Muslim republics vulnerable as well. Like the countries of the Middle East, they too are at a historic crossroads: one path leads to modernization, individual rights, separation of church and state, democracy, prosperity; the other leads to messianism, extremism, servitude, totalitarianism, irrationality, poverty.

Which path will these new countries choose? To answer this question we must first understand the growth process of fundamentalism. The social protest it represents is authentic. Long accepted and sanctified, based on a cultural legacy, it was not introduced from the outside, but evolved from within. We must therefore examine what sets this protest in motion—its patterns and its nature—before we can determine how to check its escalation.

The lamentable results of the recent Algerian elections, and even in a way of the Jordanian election, reveal a great deal. In societies that lack a modern, tiered structure, a reasonable division of national wealth, and a fairly high quality of life, even in the lower classes, autocracy will not be replaced necessarily by Western-style democracy. More likely, they will tend toward religious extremism, reflecting the yearning for a higher authority, and not for national sovereignty. The transfer from one-party rule, conservative kingship, or military government to a democracy requires combined economic and social development and guaranteed security. Otherwise, there will be no public allegiance to the new or renewed social institutions and political system. And in the absence of such allegiance, demagogues arise who exploit the public's distress, thereby gaining its support. The crisis arises from the contrast between "the language of the rights of man" and "the language of political Islam, which is totally incapable of introducing a new cultural beginning into the politics of the region."[8]

In conclusion, democratic values will not be assimilated by the public when the process of institutional democratization is not accompanied by a process of modernization, receptiveness to the outside, and social prosperity. Democracy cannot take hold in areas in which the people are unaccustomed to democratic rule and unfamiliar with the basic rights that accompany it.

THUS, economic and social development are the criteria for successful democratization of the Middle East. Sixty percent of the world's oil resources are concentrated here. The Middle East has tremendous market potential; its buildup constitutes a great challenge, and its success will open up limitless opportunities in the region. Democratization will put an end to the danger to regional and world peace. But for the democratic process to take hold, we must first overcome poverty and ignorance—the cradle of fundamentalism. The movement against modernization arises from the gap between the ethos of and economic expectations from the West, and reality. This gap is manifested in a low per capita income and GNP, hampered upward mobility, high unemployment rate, overpopulation, and limited production. The tremendous arms budget swallows any profits. The desert is spreading and the water sources are dwindling. A vicious cycle is created. It is not only "guns for socks, tanks for shoes," sung in Israel in the 1950s, not only "guns for butter," heard from generations of students of economics, but tanks for bread. This is the real problem—where it all begins. War is, after all, a tried-and-true tool for arousing patriotism, and the battle cry for country and flag suppresses criticism and controversy. However, the tremendous investment in weaponry and the concentration of knowledge and talent in the area of security come at the expense of social considerations and lead to poverty and distress, which in turn give rise to fanaticism, fundamentalism, and false messianism.

The solution to breaking this vicious cycle is clear: crush the barriers of hatred. Decide—like Israel and Egypt did so resolutely fifteen years ago—*no more war*. No more bloodshed. No more bereft parents, orphaned children, weeping widows. Peace between Israel and the Arab states and the Palestinians will eliminate an important source of tension, if not the most dangerous. Instead of visions of blood and tears there will rise visions of happiness and beauty, life and peace. We are at a historic crossroads. Do we choose the path of the tongues of fire, billowing smoke, and rivers of blood, or of blooming deserts, restored wastelands, progress, growth, justice, and freedom? The higher the standard of living rises, the lower the level of violence will fall.

3

WAR HATH NO VICTORS

UNTIL RECENTLY, THE WORLD HAD BECOME accustomed to viewing the Arab-Israeli confrontation as the principal problem in the Middle East, and Middle Eastern countries had seen the cold war as the central fact of political life, an opportunity to exploit a world conflict in order to foster regional ones. This was not the first time that local interests in this area had used a global crisis for their own ends.

But this all changed when the Arab-Israeli conflict was overshadowed by the specter of Islamic fundamentalism. Moreover, momentous events were unfolding in distant nations, and as a consequence, many of the leaders in the region were rethinking their strategies and forming new conceptions. Not only were Middle Eastern policies changing, but global policies affecting the Middle East were undergoing reform as well. During the greater part of the present century, the world had been divided both vertically and horizontally, between East and West, North and South. The former division was ideological, political, and eventually, also strategic. Communism and democracy competed for the heart of man, Russia and America for international influence, and the Warsaw Pact and NATO for the upper hand militarily. Not surprisingly, to integrate the Arab bloc into a political camp led or supported by the former Soviet Union, the Eastern bloc lavished attention on the Arab world, supplying arms under generous conditions and drawing up political doctrines in line with the goals of individual rulers. With the disintegration of the Soviet Union, the cold war came to a close, and so did its associated benefit to the conflict in the Middle East.

The division between North and South was psychological and economic, and finally, also political. The picture that emerged was one of a flourishing, progressive, scientific, and technologically oriented white North, in contrast to a poor, backward, disadvantaged, undeveloped, nonwhite South. This division led to the creation of the Nonaligned Movement (comprising 108 states—108 votes of the 160-member General Assembly) and its designation as the "Third World," as opposed to the so-called "First World." The Third World supplied the Arab nations with many votes in the United Nations and greatly enhanced their political bargaining power. However, this division, too, has become outdated. With the rising economic strength of China and India, and the economic takeoff of the so-called Asian Seven Tigers, in addition to the economic boom in Japan, Asia no longer belongs to the Third World. This is true for Latin America as well. In fact, it is totally impossible to maintain international solidarity when such solidarity derives from a division that no longer exists.

Thus, not only fundamentalism but also the absence of the automatic support from the vertical and horizontal divisions of the globe must return us to our own area—to seek peace here, to find our own sources of existence in the Middle East. The offers of yesterday disappeared with yesterday's world.

TO achieve peace, the basic problems of the Middle East need to be approached realistically. First and foremost, we must all acknowledge the futility of war: the Arabs cannot defeat Israel on the battlefield; Israel cannot dictate the conditions for peace to the Arabs. This balance of power reflects the cumulative lesson of the history of the Arab-Israeli conflict since the November 29, 1947, United Nations partition of Palestine and especially of the two wars that shaped today's grim reality: the Six-Day War in 1967 and the Yom Kippur War in 1973. In the first, the Israel Defense Forces (IDF) conducted a rapid military campaign and successfully overcame the Arab coalition. Israel broke through the blockade and astounded the world with its resounding victory . . . but it did not gain peace. Then Defense Minister Moshe Dayan waited in vain for the phone call from Arab leaders. Instead, their answer was the three no's of the Khartoum summit conference—*no* to recognition of Israel, *no* to negotiation, *no* to peace. Not many days passed before the radical Egyptian leader, President Nasser, issued the now-familiar pronouncement: "What was taken by force will not be returned, except by force." Thus, despite its definitive victory, Israel again faced grave security problems during the War of Attrition. Its lightning-quick military feat had not ensured that the Six-Day War would be its last war.

On the contrary, it was precisely this victory that sowed the seeds of the armed confrontation that was to come.

And it came.

During the Six-Day War, Israel took the other side by surprise; during the Yom Kippur War, the Egyptians and Syrians enjoyed this advantage, and the IDF was caught off-guard. The alert that sounded during the noon hours of the fateful day in 1973 abruptly ended Israel's era of tranquillity, burst the bubble of its swollen self-confidence, and reversed its often-unconscious denigration of the Arab world. Israel suffered heavy losses, and a generation of young soldiers paid with their lives to defend our homeland.

But Israel wasn't defeated yet. Even without the first-strike advantage, the IDF recovered from its initial shock and the heavy casualties and successfully halted the combined assault. The war ended with the declaration of a cease-fire, with Israeli troops well on their way to Cairo and Damascus. The billows of smoke and clouds of dust that settled over the battlefields among the dying echoes of the thunderous canons were the curtain closing on the years of steadfast Arab attempts to subdue Israel by virtue of their greater number. Were it not for Israel's later tragic and unnecessary venture into Lebanon, the Yom Kippur War could have truly been its last war. It had made a few hard truths apparent to both Israel and its neighbors: war is futile, and neither the balance of power between warring factors nor the balance of power among international interests is a guarantee of total victory.

THE immediate future holds no sign of any change in this complex balancing act. Although Israel is strong strategically and militarily, and can face down any hostile Arab coalition, even after a victory in the field, total victory—like that achieved by the Allies after World War II—is forever out of reach. Despite the end of the cold war and the breakup of the Soviet Union, heavily weighted power interests continue to play a fundamental role in the stability of the region, and neither Israel nor its enemies will be given the chance to undermine them. To every expert observer, the 1991 Persian Gulf War was the final confirmation of this inescapable fact.

Furthermore, total war—on a scale of the 1948 War of Independence—is not feasible. And a war with limited operative goals, like the Yom Kippur War, will definitely not end with the defeat of one of the warring parties, whether on the battlefield or at the negotiating table. It seems that the time for all-out war has passed. This holds true for both superpowers—which may be capable of destroying each other, but not of beating one another—and small and medium-size nations in whose stability, individually or as part of a delineated region, the superpowers have a vested interest. This is mandated by the contemporary world order as well as by today's international interdependence, the potency and ever-improving quality of modern weaponry, the snowballing financial costs of security, and the sophistication of space-age communications, which bring wars into the living room of every global village home via instant replay. The Trojan horse of war is obsolete; we each now have one of our own, in our own backyard. All these factors work together to greatly shorten the time available for strategically located or economically important smaller countries to act before direct international intervention or pressure forces them to end their attempt to shake up the system.[1] Thus, the very concept of victory should be revised, at least in connection with the Arab-Israeli conflict, to more closely resemble General Bernard Brody's analysis:

The usual conception, prevailing today almost as much as formerly . . . is preoccupied almost exclusively with the winning of wars, as though [it was] conceived to be something comparable to athletic contests—with, to be sure, an added ingredient of seriousness. The general has indeed been trained or conditioned to want desperately to win, and to be willing to pay any price possible to do so. It may be necessary to let him content himself with that conception in order that he may be the best possible *fighter,* which is the skill we mostly desire of him and the one we exclusively ask of those generals short of the very top. However, there also has to be at the top, certainly in the civilian and preferably also in the military departments of the government, the basic and prevailing conception of what any war existing or impending is really about and what it is attempting to accomplish. This attitude includes necessarily a readiness to reexamine whether under the circumstances existing it is right to continue it or whether it is better to seek some solution or termination other than victory, even if victory in the strictly military sense is judged attainable.[2]

With the Middle East at a turning point in history, it is time to seek a different "solution or termination other than victory . . . in the strictly military sense." All things considered, any war entered into now will be an unnecessary one, involving tremendous loss of life and human suffering, and so much financial and ecological damage that vast areas of the region will become desert wasteland. With no victor. There will be little or no change in basic political strategic conditions: Israel will continue to exist, and its enemies will not surrender. To be brutally honest, this type of war means the sacrifice of victims for nothing. It is bloodshed that will achieve no good purpose—except, of course, to satisfy the national need and human right of self-defense. Should there be a next war, the battles will be long and bitter, the damage will be greater than ever before, and the number of wounded both at the front and behind the lines will be unprecedented. There will be no albums or songs to laud it, and no laurels will crown the heads of the weary soldiers returning home scarred and broken in body and mind.

This message from the battlefield must guide the reasoning of Israel and its Arab neighbors. It belies the claim that we can continue endlessly in the limbo that is neither war nor peace. The Yom Kippur War proved to us all that this situation is only temporary and must end one way or another. Although as things stand now there is little to be gained from war, relations may deteriorate into war without a parallel advance toward peace. Wars don't always break out because the tacticians believe they can win. Sometimes they occur because the status quo becomes intolerable to one side—or at least less tolerable than its disruption with physical force. We might well conclude that this ambiguous status quo in and of itself harbors the seeds of calamity.

These words apply not only to us, the Israelis, but also to our Arab neighbors. However, from the Israeli viewpoint, they have another aspect—one that tips the scales. This is the fallacious interpretation of the term *territories*. Since the Six-Day War, Israelis have been disputing the future of the slivers of land we call Judea, Samaria, and the Gaza Strip and the Arabs call the West Bank and Gaza Strip. (Some Israelis have tried to introduce the Hebrew acronym of Judea, Samaria, and Gaza Strip, *Yeshah,* which means "salvation," because of its obvious connotations.) Some see them as "liberated territories," others as "occupied territories." Still others prefer the more neutral "administrated territories." All are incorrect. There is no point in discussing geography while ignoring demography. The word *territories* is meaningless when such "territories" are inhabited. The Sinai Desert is a territory: it is almost completely uninhabited. Egypt used it for mobilization of troops, and after the Six-Day War Israel used the land for the same purpose until it was returned to Egypt, in accordance with the peace agreement and to cement the peace. The other areas that came under Israeli rule in the wake of the Six-Day War are not territories. The Gaza Strip has an area of 365 square kilometers (140 square miles), with a population of roughly 800,000. Gaza is not a territory: it is not only settled, it hits world records in population density. Those who speak of the territories without considering the Palestinians residing there are shutting their own eyes and throwing sand in the eyes of the public. The territories are not the problem with which we must deal, but our future relationship with their inhabitants is. And those who speak of annexation of the territories really mean annexation of their people, with all the long-term demographic and political implications for the entire national future of Israel, its identity as the one state of the Jewish nation, and its democratic government. It is not by accident that even when the Likud government was the Israeli controlling party, Judea, Samaria, and Gaza were not annexed; only the very sparsely populated Golan Heights was.

NOT only has war become purposeless, but the desire to govern and control another nation is no longer feasible. Indeed, we never intended to become the rulers of another people. The *intifada* highlighted the abyss between "us" and "them." A second factor is the significance of such control in the eyes of the Israelis. The IDF has been forced to become, in effect, a garrison—a local governing power. Its highly praised soldiers skirmish with local citizens and children in the alleyways of the refugee camps in

Gaza and the Casbah in Nablus, provoked by stone-throwing Palestinian youths, and at the mercy of masked hoodlums charging through the streets, brandishing knives and guns and hurling invectives against the military rule of Israel. With their live ammunition and blades, these youths are living proof of the senselessness of the status quo, which was designed to enforce Israeli security.

The war with Lebanon generated an essential change in the quality of power relations between Israel and the Palestinians. At the onset of the Arab-Israeli conflict, the Palestine Liberation Organization (PLO) and other similar groups employed pure terror tactics. They only attacked the defenseless—children on their way to school, captive bus passengers, field workers. Ordinary citizens sitting peacefully in their own homes suddenly found themselves under Katyusha attacks or subject to terrorist acts coming from the sea. Until the war with Lebanon, these organizations dared not attack IDF targets, military units, or secure bases.

The turnabout came when, as a result of misguided decisions on the part of the Israeli government, led astray by its own ambitions to create a strategic change in the area by invading Lebanon, the IDF found itself engaged in a direct battle with the PLO and other irregular forces. The army placed its full operative power into its attack, integrating all ground, air, and sea forces and using sophisticated equipment and primitive strategic policy. This created the impression that it was a war between equals. This was no longer a police action against outlaw terrorists who were ruthlessly trampling international law, but a battle between two armed camps. With astonishing shortsightedness, the Israeli government of the day ignored the moral advantage of the IDF—an advantage that has always been one of the main components of the national strength of the Jewish state.

Although the war forced the PLO to retreat from Lebanon, it did not remove it from the national arena or as the decisive factor setting the tone for the Palestinian front. And in the shade of the cedar trees, and beneath the cherry blossoms, the seeds of the *intifada* and of Israeli recognition of the need for bilateral talks were planted.

L I K U D rhetoric could not change anything. Although the Likud party had sworn that it would never, under any circumstances, sit down at the negotiating table with a terrorist organization, it was in fact former Prime Minister Yitzhak Shamir who headed the Israeli delegation to Madrid in 1991. In his autobiography, George Shultz, who served as Secretary of State under President Reagan, repeated his claim, with complete authority, that after the reported meeting between King Hussein and myself in London, little was needed to reach the first peace agreement with Jordan and the Palestinians. But Mr. Shamir undermined the process, the *intifada* broke out, and eventually it took the intensive mediation of James Baker, Secretary of State under President Bush, to get Shamir to attend the international conference in Madrid. The conference, which Shamir had objected to from the outset, included a Palestinian delegation that derived its authority from the PLO leadership in Tunis. Thus, despite its sententious and weak denials, it was the Likud that started indirect negotiations with the PLO. True, the Shamir administration did everything in its power to cripple the process it had started. This two-faced action explains the Likud attitude toward peace and the propagandist use it makes of the national yearning for peace. But the Likud was unable to erase the glaring fact that it had begun the negotiations with Tunis-controlled Palestinian representatives. The Likud had so derided the "Jordanian option" and the "London document" that it found itself sitting face-to-face with Dr. Haddar al-Shafi, a founder of the PLO and one of the formulators of the Palestinian pact—the same document the Likud cites as evidence of the pointlessness in discussing peace with the PLO.

What a bitter historical irony. There would have been no need for the Madrid process or negotiations with so particularist a Palestinian delegation had Likud leaders not persisted in rejecting the 1987 London agreement with King Hussein to open direct negotiations under the aegis of an international conference. The entire process would have begun long ago, before the *intifada* ever began, and the Palestinians would have been represented by a joint Jordanian-Palestinian delegation. The chances for peace would have been greater and Israel's relative bargaining position more favorable. We could have avoided the need to negotiate with a Palestinian-only delegation controlled by PLO headquarters if only Likud leaders had not been blindsided by pipe dreams and an impossible political ideal in whose name they were prepared to wreak havoc with the most significant breakthrough since Sadat's visit to Jerusalem.

The stubbornness and shortsightedness of the Likud leadership led to complex entanglements, and the *intifada* exposed the IDF to unprecedented difficulties. Historians will justify the behavior of Israeli soldiers and commanders when faced with such an unorthodox situation—a situation no army could train for and none could be expected to stand for, either operationally or morally.

In his *Utopia,* Sir Thomas More described the effect a long state of siege has on those of the conquering nation, in this example the Achorians:

Long ago, these people went to war to gain another realm
for their king, who had inherited an ancient claim to it

through marriage. When they had conquered it, they soon saw that keeping it was going to be as hard as getting it had been. Their new subjects were continually rebelling or being attacked by foreign invaders, the Achorians had to be constantly at war for them or against them, and they saw no hope of ever being able to disband their army. In the meantime, they were being heavily taxed, money flowed out of their kingdom, their blood was being shed for the advantage of others, and peace was no closer than it ever was. The war corrupted their own citizens by encouraging lust for robbery and murder; and the laws fell into contempt.[3]

In the sixteenth century, More foresaw that such a process would ultimately cause the king to make concessions on that same kingdom, not because he was relinquishing his rights but because continuation of the status quo would be untenable for both the population and himself. Instead of working for the good of his nation, the ruler must summon all his resources to fend off the perpetual threat of war, from within and without.

Twenty-six years after Israel's victory in a war forced upon it, which forced the country to establish military rule in the territories, we can use More's description to reach certain conclusions about the relationship the State of Israel has with the Palestinians. Israel is now administering two parallel governmental systems with contradictory sets of values. By its very nature, the military government is oppressive—to the people it rules and to the citizens of the state. It is the very antithesis of the basic, democratic values set down in Israel's Declaration of Independence, in our basic laws, our political culture, and in our social-world view. Zionism arose to right the injustices inflicted on the Jews, and to give the Jews basic human rights. Therefore, our coercive rule of another nation and forcible control of public order in an area under military rule affects not only the performance of the governmental authorities in the territories but also those in the heartland of Israel itself—just as More predicted. Although our intention was to quash terrorist activities, the very existence of a military government is enough to generate negative feelings. These are not extended to the General Security Service (GSS), whose members demonstrate a fierce sense of duty and take tremendous personal risks to combat murder and sabotage, and who have saved many Jewish and Arab lives. Rather, the main complaint is aimed at the situation itself, which invites animosity on both sides. A nation that forces itself on another nation, even for reasons of self-defense, loses the will to abstain from oppression because of the dynamics of conquest—a part of the same "invisible hand" that regulates history.

THERE is no sense in preserving the status quo. Not for Israel, not for the Palestinians. The Palestinians cannot defeat Israel, and organized or ad hoc terrorist acts, bombing, kidnappings, hijackings, and stabbings will not blow out Israel's national flame. We are a determined people, and no power on earth can make us leave this land after fifty generations of living in the Diaspora, fifty generations of oppression and suffering and genocide. We will not move from the only place on earth where we can renew our independence, achieve security, and live with self-respect and honor— our honor, and our neighbors'. We want to establish a true neighborly relationship with our neighbors.

Israel has no short- or long-term interest in ruling the Palestinians or in viewing them as "hostages" to the war situation, a situation we indeed want to end. Maintaining the present situation is pointless, and, owing to a high birth rate and immigration, the status quo cannot continue in any case. Recognizing the hard truth is a criterion for the success of the peace process—without victors, without victims. War does not solve any problems; peace is the solution. As the results of our accord with Egypt have shown, we can have a peaceful relationship with our neighbors. By compromising—minimum concessions and maximum justice on both sides—we will live to see the day when nations are free of the sorrow of war, including our own nation as well.

4

THE REGIONAL SYSTEM

PEACE BETWEEN ISRAEL AND ITS ARAB NEIGH-bors will create the environment for a basic reorganization of Middle Eastern institutions. Reconciliation and Arab acceptance of Israel as a nation with equal rights and responsibilities will sire a new sort of cooperation—not only between Israel and its neighbors but also among Arab nations. It will change the face of the region and its ideological climate.

The problems of this region of the world cannot be solved by individual nations, or even on a bilateral or multilateral plane. Regional organization is the key to peace and security, and will promote democratization, economic development, national growth, and individual prosperity. But this change will not come with the wave of a magic wand or a diplomatic sleight of hand. Establishing peace and security requires a conceptual revolution. It is not a simple task, but it is essential; otherwise, what equanimity we do achieve will be short-lived.

Our ultimate goal is the creation of a regional community of nations, with a common market and elected centralized bodies, modeled on the European Community. The need for this regional framework is based on four fundamental factors:

Political Stability

Fundamentalism is rapidly making its way deeply into every Arab country in the Middle East, endangering regional peace as well as individual government stability. One of the main perpetrators of this growth is the Western media; the extremists also maintain ultranational communications networks, exploiting the very technology they claim to despise. With no religious law outlawing the use of public communications, fundamentalists have learned to use the media to their own advantage. Their campaigns employ popular symbols and high-level propaganda to lure activists and supporters. An organized response to this threat is imperative to preserve freedom, peace, and political stability. The answer, then, is a systematized regional structure that will introduce a new framework for the region and that will provide the potential for economic and social growth, extinguishing the fire of religious extremism and cooling the hot winds of revolution.[1]

Economics

A higher standard of living is a precondition for mitigating the tensions among Middle Eastern countries. As long as there is a gap between people's expectations and the opportunities within the sociopolitical system, there will be space for fundamentalism to develop. Today, no struggling economy can grow without receiving outside assistance or becoming part of a broad regional system. A cooperative regional organization that acts on an ultra-national forum is the answer—the only answer—to fundamentalism. Moreover, only an umbrella organization will be capable of establishing the shared high-tech irrigation system necessary to check the growth of the desert and to enable countries to produce enough food and jobs for their population. Only a practical, regional approach can fully exploit the potential for tourism and public communications in this rich area of the world, making the region prosperous for its people.

National Security

In an age of ground-to-ground missiles and nuclear capability, a regional system of surveillance and oversight is the only means of ensuring a reasonable level of national security. Iraq's use of chemical weapons during the Iran-Iraq War and to suppress a Kurdish uprising, and its deployment of ground-to-ground missiles directed at Israel and Saudi Arabia during the Persian Gulf War, are proof that traditional strategic concepts are almost obsolete. As we approach the twenty-first century, "strategic depth" has little meaning. Long-range ballistic missiles and weapons of mass destruction have turned the home front into the front line. Israel's 1981 bombing of Iraq's nuclear power plant and the U.S. bombing a decade later did not end the region's nuclear threat—it merely gave us a brief respite. Today, research-and-development efforts for a nuclear capability have been resumed, conducted in easy-to-conceal underground facilities. Iraq has taught us that while brilliant military campaigns may destroy nuclear generators, they cannot eradicate an iron will or evil intentions. At best, wars delay the danger, and sometimes they exacerbate it. To overcome the nuclear threat, we in the Middle East must imitate the sane approach of the superpowers: at the height of the cold war, not satisfied by their "balance of fear," they realized that cooperation was essential, and arms control and arms reduction became the call of the day. So, too, a mutually beneficial regional security framework will highlight the limitations of nuclear power, especially as more and more countries obtain increasingly sophisticated machinery. The regional alliance will help prevent someone from pushing that fateful button, after which there will be nothing.

Democratization

The Middle East needs democracy as much as a human needs oxygen. Democracy is not only a process that guarantees personal and civil freedom but also is a watchdog for peace, working to dispel the factors that underlie fundamentalist agitation. Regional democratization means communications development. By attacking "pathological" conditions within a nation without attacking the nation itself, a country's media can help make democracy triumph. This victory is the best guarantee of a durable peace: democratic nations do not enter into war with one another. Likewise, totalitarianism has proved to be costly and inefficient. It requires a large secret police force, a spit-and-polish army, and constant censorship. Citizens live in constant fear. Totalitarianism paralyzes initiative and closes borders. It invites protest, but hurries to suppress it, thereby creating more bitterness and unrest. A Syrian poet in exile, Nazar Kabany, wrote the following lines: "Would a bird need the permission of the Interior Ministry to fly / and would a fish need a permit to swim / we would live in a world where birds couldn't fly and fish couldn't swim." [N.p., n.d.]

Ultimately, only a democratic system will allow for long-term prosperity and economic growth, as well as national and personal security. A regional system will generate competition by adopting democratic processes, preventing an internal threat to governments, and eliminating the implied challenge to other nations. Democratization in and of itself has the power of renewal. And the need for governmental renewal is especially apparent in the Middle East, which has more autocratic rulers than any other region in the world. Unfortunately, it is this very fact that lowers the chances that democracy will take hold here. Moreover, the presence of fundamentalism, an essentially antidemocratic movement even when it uses democratic slogans, makes it even more difficult to introduce democratic processes. A regional framework, on the other hand, will at least ease some military tension, assisting the democratic process to take hold.

The introduction of a regional system is dependent on the success of the Arab-Israeli peace process. To be more precise, the proposed regional system will evolve along with the predetermined two-phase peace process. Security—the prevention of war and the establishment of a secure, bilateral order—will be the dominant issue in the first, or transitory, phase. Geographic lines will reflect security considerations along with demographic, historical, economic, and political factors. This was true in our accord with Egypt and in our agreement with Syria in the mid-1970s. The matter of security also applies to the autonomy plan with the Palestinians, with the latter based not on designated land but on a timetable. I've heard it said that a pier is a frustrated bridge. Until now there was an Israeli pier and a Palestinian pier. We intend to build a bridge of time, a bridge of five years, that will connect the two piers and put an end to the frustration. Thus, the main aim of this first phase of the peace process is to decrease

friction and eliminate the sources of hostility by establishing mutual trust and a willingness to consider the future. It is a transitory
phase—a passage from one step to the next—in a journey with a
clear destination. Even security arrangements cannot take hold if
there has been no time limit set. As the bitter lessons of the Yom
Kippur War have taught us, temporary arrangements crumble if
not replaced by permanent provisions.

Can the two sides meet on the bridge of autonomy and advance toward a permanent arrangement? In the second, decisive,
phase of the peace process the specific nature of the peace is the
dominant issue. The principal goal is to establish a stable system
of good neighborly relations. The ensuing equable and secure environment will, in turn, lead to growth, development, prosperity,
and well-being—for every person, every nation, the entire region.
This phase will center on long-term considerations such as nor-
malization of relations, establishment of economic and cultural
ties, and determination of permanent and reasonable borders.
Preferably these borders will be determined by national aspirations (history and demographics), not by security considerations
alone. After all, a stable and durable peace will, in itself, enhance
security. Toward this end, we must cultivate general interest in
maintaining the peace, and convince all parties to embrace a new
and different way to contemplate the future of the region and the
future of each Middle Eastern nation. On this basis, we can also
foster recognition of our common fate and show how a realistic
approach serves all. These goals add a new dimension to the concept of an Arab-Israeli peace, beyond simply ending the state of
war. "Peace," said Spinoza, "is not the absence of war, it is a
virtue, a state of mind, a disposition for benevolence, confidence,
justice."[2] Thus, the plan for Palestinian autonomy essentially sev-
ers the past from the present. This design for a new Middle East is
a passageway to a new future for all.

REGIONAL SECURITY

The Middle East regional security system will be structured around two types of mutual obligation: nation-to-nation (bilateral and multilateral) and nation-to-region. The direct nation-to-nation arrangements will serve, in and of themselves, as a deterrent to aggression. The duties charged by the regional security system will help enforce the peace, because only a regional framework will allow a dismantling of power structures, work toward disarmament, and control of trigger-happy fingers. The regional program will implement a system to collect data on military activities and report to all sides. To ensure long-term stability, the system will also employ space satellites, in collaboration with the superpowers.

We are not aiming for a NATO-like system for defense against a common, external enemy. After peace has been achieved, the main security problems in the Middle East will be intrasystem instability, political sabotage, and backsliding into the seemingly indestructible network of religious, ethnic, and economic hostilities. The regional security system is designed to keep the lid on this Pandora's box: to prevent a war that could arise from a short-circuit in communications and to plant the new political order in firm ground.

This new concept of regional security differs in several important respects from the group security system the Allies tried to implement after World War I. The Western nations failed miserably because of their helplessness in the face of fascist aggression, having had no means of collecting information or of guarding the peace, and lacking the support of friendly countries outside of Europe. They naïvely assumed, in keeping with the antimilitarist zeitgeist of postwar Europe, that when the test came, all nations would mobilize to defeat the aggressor.[3] As a result, the Allies closed their eyes and their minds to the looming fascist threat. Allied paralysis in 1936 undermined the peace treaty (although on the face of it, the truce remained effective for another three years).[4] The events that followed were a direct result of astonishing Western shortsightedness, a refusal to acknowledge facts that contradicted the hope that there would be no more wars, not even for peace. Winston Churchill, an ordinary Member of Parliament at the time, saw it coming. In response to Hitler's invasion of the Rhine Valley in violation of the treaty, he wrote, "If no means of lawful redress can be offered to the aggrieved party, the whole doctrine of international law and co-operation upon which the hopes of the future are based would lapse ignominiously. It would be replaced immediately by a system of alliances and groups of nations deprived of all guarantees but their own right arm."[5]

The events of the thirties teach us three lessons. First, to prevent a tactical surprise, we must establish independent supervisory bodies that have the power and ability to act when necessary. The arrangement in Sinai—under which an international mediatory force acts in accordance with the Israel-Egypt peace accords —could serve as a model here. Factors relevant to the specific circumstances must, of course, be taken into consideration. The force will operate on a bilateral basis under the auspices of the regional system.

Second, to further protect the region against a tactical surprise and to nip in the bud any sudden aggressive actions, we should conduct routine surveillance, providing regular reports to the friendly superpowers. These reports will include satellite information, as discussed earlier. This broad control of military movements is a logical replacement for the concept of "strategic depth." On a broad strategic level, the report will also include research and development.

Third, in the event that diplomatic channels temporarily break down during a crisis, the region must have troops that can respond immediately and effectively to aggression. Unfortunately, the vision of prophets Isaiah and Micah, "nation shall not lift up sword against nation, neither shall they learn war any more" (Isaiah 2:4; Micah 4:3), still eludes us. We continue to learn war. But we no longer do so in order to declare war; we do so to keep the peace and thwart aggression. A cautious and timely Roman proverb teaches: "Let him who desires peace, prepare for war."[6] The time has not yet come to dismantle our weapons and send our soldiers home. We dare not revert to the naïveté of postwar Western leaders. We can, however, institute a gradual long-term process of reciprocal disarmament. This will foster trust among cooperating nations and enforce the authority of the regional system.

REGIONAL ECONOMICS

The concept of a regional economy involves the step-by-step establishment of a community of nations, much like the European Community. Western Europe's nations had a deep-rooted historical hatred for one another, which, in some cases, endured centuries longer than has the conflict between the Arab countries and Israel. However, these European nations did not negate their neighbor's right to exist. In this respect, the Arab-Israeli friction is far more vitriolic. Toward the end of World War II, few Western Europeans believed that a common market could be established in the not-too-distant future or that a sovereign European Community would be formed, even vested with the authority to act against the interests of one or more of its members, and providing its proud citizens with an ultranational identity.

In 1948, French author Jean-Jacques Servan-Schreiber visited Germany. At the time, he was a correspondent for the daily *Le Monde* in France. Forty years later, he published a book in which he summarized his impressions of Germany and some conversations that took place upon his return home:

> I came back very upset. Will the Germans be left defeated, unarmed, humiliated? Should we not use this unique opportunity to establish a historical system of communications? On my return from Germany I put in a request through my editor to interview the first President of France after World War II, Vincent Auriol, who was a socialist. I explained to him what I thought was our golden opportunity. "Let us suggest to the Germans," I said, "an equal partnership with France in the unification of Europe." I still remember every word that greeted my ears from that statesman, who was wise and trustworthy, despite the contents of his reply to me during that conversation: "I like your noble ideas, my young friend, but you are in too much of a hurry. We cannot achieve such a thing so soon after the great tragedy of this war. Wounds need time to heal. In twenty years we might suppose you will be right, and your generation will be able to advance towards this task. Today, no one will understand, and we are liable only to ruin its prospects. Wait patiently."
>
> Several weeks later I met Jean Monnet, a different kind of statesman, enthusiastic about national change. He was at the time only a representative for planning in France, but he was even more excited and impatient than me in his desire to start working towards a French-German conciliation. Standing before the huge map of Europe on his wall, a

prominent circle drawn around France and Germany, he graced me with a lovely, very organized lecture. A few weeks later he established the Coal and Steel Fund, which thereafter became a "cooperative market" and opened the way towards a unified Europe. His vision was the one proven correct, and not the old, traditional one.[7]

I, too, met with Jean Monnet in the 1950s. He told me that he had envisioned the European market as not merely economic but also political. To make this vision a reality required statistical data, not political rhetoric. Politicians, he told me with a smile, have a greater tendency to engage in polemics than to wade through statistics.

The Middle East needs a Jean Monnet approach today. We need courage and forethought, imagination and insight. We must move away from the age-old sureties that assume, "The thing that hath been, it is that which shall be; and that which is done is that which shall be done; and there is no new thing under the sun" (Ecclesiastes 1:9). This belief gives credence to unimaginative, passive thinkers who cannot lift the veil of the future and see the new, burgeoning reality. Today more than ever, we need men and women with novel ideas and creative concepts—leaders unafraid of the hardships encountered in building a brave new world. David Ben-Gurion said that all experts are experts on what already was. We need experts on what will be.

True, in the 1950s, France and West Germany faced a common enemy, and this helped them overcome their hostility to one another, the residue of centuries-old hatreds and the wounds of terrible wars. That enemy was, of course, Stalinist Russia, which threatened to spread westward and destroy their freedom and well-being. It was this setting, coupled with a mutual abhorrence of war, that enabled the leaders of these nations and their Western European allies to overcome the past for the good of the future.

In the Middle East, we too have a common enemy: poverty. The father of fundamentalism, poverty is a threat to progress, development, freedom, and prosperity. We have much to lose if we do not establish a regional framework that will vanquish the prophets of doom. And we have so much to gain, if only we know how to bridge the abyss of blood and tears—if we look forward in hope, not back in anger.

A true leadership is chosen by the people of today, in order to represent the electorate of tomorrow—those citizens who have not yet been given the right to choose. Elected by the parents, we must serve the children. We must use the classic strategies familiar to graduates of military academies. Start by defining the ultimate goal and then work backward, establishing interim goals and allocating the proper tools to reach them. We cannot advance via trial and error, without a clear understanding of where we are going and what we aim to achieve. Improvisation will get us nowhere. Our plan must be professional, well reasoned, and well formulated, so that it can steer us in the right direction, turning theory into productive policy.

Some claim that, even in Europe, the era of nationalism has not yet come to a close. The Middle East, to which the modern concept of nationalism arrived a bit late, has a powerful history that is liable to hinder the establishment of a regional community. Does this mean that we must give up such a promising plan? No. If we cannot do it in a single step, we will proceed in stages. We might describe the plan as a three-tiered pyramidal program of cooperation. The first stage will include binational or multinational projects, such as a joint research institute for desert management or cooperative desalination plants. The ongoing productive cooperation between Israel and Egypt in agriculture is a good example of this approach. Projects may even be put into effect before a permanent peace is established. Israel already has mutual economic and research programs with various countries with which it has not as yet signed peace treaties.

The second stage will involve international consortiums, which will carry out projects requiring large capital investments, under the supervision of relevant countries in the region and perhaps other interested parties as well. Examples of such projects are a Red Sea–Dead Sea canal coupled with development of free trade and tourism along its length; a joint Israeli–Jordanian–Saudi Arabian port; development of hydroelectric power for electricity and desalination; and well-planned, rapid development of Dead Sea industries. When these desert projects are completed, they will fulfill Ben-Gurion's dream of developing the Negev, opening new horizons for countries of the region and creating real interest in preserving the peace.

The third stage will include regional community policy, with gradual development of official institutions. Our era has witnessed the emergence of two contradictory trends: particularist nationalism and ultranational development of regional communities. In every area in which the first has staked a claim, the social order has been subverted and hostility and violence have taken root. The areas of the former country of Yugoslavia are a prime example of this. In contrast, everywhere the ultranational trend predominates, there is sensitivity to human needs, opportunities, and desires, leading to a more lasting international order that strives for prosperity, development, and human rights. Western Europe is a shining example of this.

Beyond the particularist nationalist aspirations, nations of the region constitute a heterogeneous conglomeration of socioeconomic levels, standards of living, and per capita income. To overcome this problem, we need to view the region as wrapped in four economic-political belts. The first belt is disarmament. The Middle East today spends approximately $60 billion on arms annually. If we cut this by half, we will have huge monies for development of the entire region, without infringing upon the national security of an individual member nation.

The second belt is water, biotechnology, and the war against the desert. It aims to paint the Middle East green, to supply abundant food for its many inhabitants.

The third belt is a transportation and communications infrastructure. Every common market hinges on the relative benefit of geographic proximity; in the absence of an appropriate infrastructure, however, this is only a theoretical advantage.

And the fourth belt is tourism. Tourism is an important industry, which can, in a relatively short time, generate profits and create employment opportunities. By building temples and pyramids, forts and aqueducts, our forefathers bequeathed us fabulous tourist attractions. Tourism also has political value, because it both requires and imposes tranquillity. A flourishing and stable tourist industry is also good for security—equal in importance to an international police force.

Leaders in the Middle East today shoulder a great responsibility. They can follow the road paved by Western Europe, or they can emulate the hatred of the Balkans. Moving from a strategy of military superiority to one of economic cooperation will help us choose the correct path, and future generations will thank us.

5

THE BASIS FOR SECURITY
A New Way of Thinking

DURING HIS HISTORIC NOVEMBER 1977 VISIT to Jerusalem, Egyptian President Anwar el-Sadat hoped to break the psychological barrier to peace. And indeed, when the president of the largest and strongest Arab country made an official visit to the capital of Israel, many barriers did fall. As part of that peace settlement, our troops withdrew to the international line drawn during the period of the British Mandate.

Today, it is difficult to envision a leader taking such a dramatic step. Our young soldiers, on both sides of the line, are the third and fourth generation taking part in an ongoing conflict, educated toward a specific set of images, preconceptions, and stereotypes.

Almost invariably, each side associates the other with ill intent, usually the worst possible motives. Therefore, they expect any peace accord to reflect their suspicions, which are based on past experiences and their frequently distorted picture of reality. Moreover, peace with Syria and the Palestinians is on the horizon. Think of it! Peace with the most bitter enemies ever known to Israel, whom Israeli leaders have described as the devil incarnate because of their alleged desire to push us into the sea. Many Israelis continue to view Syrians and Palestinians as uncompromising enemies, who plan to destroy us in stages after they have failed to do so in one fell swoop. And on the Palestinian side, we hear the voices of the Cassandras, who attribute only malicious intent to the Israelis, who refuse to learn from past mistakes, and who reject the hand extended in peace.

When Israelis and Arabs come to the negotiating table with the belief that those sitting opposite have only malevolent motives, they belie the purity of their own intentions. They also show a lack in moral strength to overcome the psychological barriers. As long as images of the past threaten our present efforts to build a new future, we will get nowhere. We will sentence ourselves to an endless cycle of wars and bloodshed, to the pointless sacrifice of young victims, to a world without hope. Those who ideologically or psychologically will not or cannot restructure their thinking to the new reality will be unable to guarantee a secure future for their country. After all, what is the value of security that only carries us back to the battlefield?

Breaking that psychological barrier is the precondition for success in our quest for peace and prosperity in the Middle East. The two sides must learn to see each other as people—to understand each other's desires and doubts, hopes and fears. This is not an easy task, but it is essential for harmony and security. And the process will also give us an overview of our basic problems. National security, of course, heads this list.

AFTER hundreds of years of brutal hostilities, the Middle East must be fully aware of the significance of peace. Not only are political, defense, and economic patterns destined to change but our thought patterns are as well. We must awaken to this revolutionary significance of peace in a region that has known only war. The factors, principles, and presumptions of defense and strategic policy, which worked in wartime and during endless training for "the next round," must be adapted to the new situation or abolished altogether, not only on the regional level but also on the national level. The very fact of an established peace forces us to reexamine the basic premises of our defense policy.

For instance, the peace accord will lay the groundwork for the superstructure that will provide security for all people and all nations of the Middle East. It is only the first step, and under no circumstances will it be the final one. Even after the treaty has been signed and demilitarization, disarmament, and control measures have been put into effect, nations will still need armies. Their presence will simultaneously increase security in individual countries and lower the level of regional security. Thus, the principal strategic problem Middle Eastern leaders face now is how to upgrade national security without decreasing regional security. This issue will become even more vital as technology advances, and we find ourselves increasingly dependent on regional security as the guarantor of national and personal security.

To clarify these developments and specify the basic assumptions involved in formulating a new perception of security, we must first reexamine some traditional concepts. "Strategic depth"

may no longer have the same meaning when peaceful relations
and reciprocal control systems are in effect. Strategic areas do not
have the same value in peacetime as they do in war. The significance of military campaigns and tactical considerations changes
when armed conflict is replaced by equable, amiable relationships.
Military strategists will continue to take these factors into account;
but when leaders formulate a new defense policy, they will
reevaluate these criteria vis-à-vis the many other considerations
that constitute a new national defense policy.

In the past, soldiers were the ones exposed to danger in a war;
today, large populated areas are the main target. Any use of ballistic missiles in the next war could turn the Middle East into a
post-blitz London, Rotterdam, Warsaw, Leipzig, or Hamburg. As
already noted, we have no adequate military means to neutralize
this threat, and therefore, we must instill a new concept of re-
gional-based security.

Indeed, our new approach to security in the region is not limited to geography and topography. We have to alter our assumptions in accordance with changes in the world order and the role
of the superpowers as well as consider modern technological developments. We must revise our general concept of war as a tool
of international relations. Classical strategy depended on three
components: time, space, and quantity. The new military technology questions the importance of these elements. What value
does time have if a ground-to-ground missile travels from Washington to Moscow in only six minutes? What significance do
physical barriers—mountains, rivers, deserts—have when missiles
can fly over or around them toward their predetermined targets?
In the face of nuclear, chemical, and biological warfare, what
advantage do we reap from having hundreds of tanks, cannons,
and jets?

When the superpowers saw the implications of these questions, they realized their wars were obsolete. The United States and the Soviet Union did, however, continue to develop and produce conventional weapons, and the battlefields of the Middle East served as a giant testing ground for advanced military technology. Over the years, the major world powers were involved, to a greater or lesser extent, in various regional conflicts—Vietnam, Afghanistan, Africa, and the Middle East—but no direct war was declared between these bitter political and ideological opponents.

Strong countries with nuclear capability try not to be pulled into conventional wars, either. This was especially clear when Nikita Khrushchev decided to accept John F. Kennedy's ultimatum during the 1962 Cuban Missile Crisis. An awareness that these weapons have the potential to annihilate the entire world has forced the superpowers to act in a rational manner, even at the height of the cold war. Eventually the proliferation of these weapons of mass destruction forced nations to find a political substitute, such as disarmament, limitations on production and testing, and a ban on exploding unconventional warheads. This was true even in the face of severe hatred, which fifty years earlier would have terminated in an all-out war between the Eastern and Western blocs, with active participation by the United States and the Soviet Union.

The struggle between the superpowers to control the Middle East began to wane even before the fall of communism, a result of the Soviet Union's economic difficulties and its policy of granting Middle Eastern countries military aid without financial return. Since the demise of the Soviet Union, there has been no global confrontation in the Middle East. That power play, which financed the weapons industries in both blocs, was the incentive for repeated wars that did not solve any problems. Now, it seems, the message has come through loud and clear: more wars mean more victims, but no more solutions. It is also clear that foreign powers no longer have an interest in provoking one side or another in this tumultuous and sensitive region. Maintaining a modern army and continuing the arms race will only destroy the economy and invite disquiet. The international political setting is no longer conducive to war, and the threat of growing poverty forces us in the Middle East to find new means for achieving our national objectives.

ESTABLISHMENT of a regional security system depends on recognition of the one fact that distinguishes the final years of the twentieth century: national political organizations can no longer fulfill the purpose for which they were established—that is, to furnish the fundamental needs of the nation. Since time immemorial, people have formed sociopolitical units to work together to supply basic needs and guarantee security. This is still true today. Outside of an organized, established social framework, people cannot provide for security and produce what they need for daily survival. Thus, personal security is tied to and depends on collective security. And besides offering physical comfort and security, the group facilitates communication with others, leading to self-awareness. Like personal security, individual identity is linked inexorably to collective identity. This association between identity and security is so intimate that often people are forced to endanger their own security for the good of the group. In many cases, people offer to do so of their own free will. This is the essence of national military service: individuals contribute their time and freedom, and even endanger their lives and health, to defend the public.

In light of contemporary technological developments—those both for construction and for destruction—a nationwide organization is not sufficient to ensure this security. The social group has expanded, and today our health, welfare, and freedom can be ensured only within a wider framework, on a regional or even an ultraregional basis. One day our self-awareness and personal identity will be based on this new reality, and we will find that we have stepped outside the national arena. Western Europe is already showing signs of this new age. (In a way, it is following the American example. After all, the American Colonies were a historic attempt to build an improved Europe.) But the road is long and difficult, and even in the West people sometimes take two steps backward for every step forward. In the Middle East, as in Eastern Europe, the process is more complex; people are not yet ready to accept an ultranational identity.

Despite this reality, there is constantly growing demand for a new political entity responsible for a broader-based security. Will this need dictate the direction history will take? Will far-reaching economic and security considerations overcome psychological obstinacy?

In the past, the central issue of the Arab-Israeli conflict was the Palestinian problem. This is no longer true; now it is the nuclear threat, reflected by the biggest change taking place in our world. Up to now, major conflicts have erupted between nations or countries. The response to these international disputes has been mustering an army, formulating a strategy, and, after hopes of finding a diplomatic solution were exhausted, entering the battlefield. Today, there is no military answer to the nuclear threat. There is no military answer to poverty and fundamentalism. There is no military answer to radical terrorism. There is no military answer to ecological disaster. We live in a world of new problems and old strategies. These old strategies are incapable of solving the new problems; indeed, they have been known to aggravate them.

With the dissolution of the Soviet Union, the West lost an old enemy but gained a host of new problems. It is simpler to fight an enemy than to solve problems; opposing Khrushchev was easier than aiding Yeltsin. An enemy can be identified: we know where he can be found, how strong he is, what weapons he has, what methods he uses in battle, and what level of threat he poses. These missions, difficult as they seem, are much easier than identifying a problem, locating its source, determining its strength, and estimating when it is going to get out of hand. We are in transition from a world of identifiable enemies to one of unidentifiable problems.

Maintaining a modern army is an expensive undertaking and creates the desire for modern weaponry. Yet this cycle only intensifies a nation's poverty. And missiles do not respect borders, do not give more than a few minutes' warning, and are almost impossible to stop en route. The investment necessary to build an antiballistic missile system is so great that success will not automatically translate to a buildup of power. When these missiles have unconventional warheads, they become so deadly that they threaten the entire world's very existence. Counting the number of existing missiles with nuclear warheads is absurd, because the destruction caused by even one may be absolute. Small and medium-size countries, where essential resources are concentrated along accessible arteries or which contain few distant densely populated enclaves, are particularly vulnerable. As long as the enemy has second-strike capacity, a country can only hope that its rational opponent will behave as the superpowers did during the cold war. But what to do if it is an irrational enemy, a fanatic Ayatollah or fervent terrorist, who draws strength and courage from a vision of "apocalypse now" and who is prepared to sacrifice the entire world if his demands are not met?

Our greatest danger today is from the combination of nuclear weapons and extremist ideology. To this, I repeat, there is not and can never be an acceptable military answer. The concept of deterrence that would be relevant to this type of ideologist deviates so sharply from what would be tolerable to the rest of humanity that the outcome is hard to imagine. We must also take into account the possibility that nuclear weapons may fall into irresponsible hands.

Thus, we must conclude that the modern era offers no foolproof means of national defense other than a wide-ranging regional arrangement. Moreover, national security hinges on this regional security. Eventually, we will need global defense, because the fundamentalist movement has designs on even the far corners of the earth. Only an authoritative, regional political coalition can save the Middle East and its nations from the lethal combination of nuclear power and fundamentalism. We have far to go, but in light of the unprecedented danger, we must amass our intellectual resources and overcome our irrational obstacles. And we must start immediately.

AN ounce of prevention is worth a pound of cure: foiling a threat is better than winning a war. The best way to mitigate the dual dangers of modern weaponry and age-old poverty is to mobilize our resources and technical tools to uncouple this combination, fighting poverty as if it were a military threat. To save the future of the Middle East and provide its residents with security, it is not enough to settle differences bilaterally or even multilaterally. We must build a new Middle East. Within this framework, peace is the means for security, not just as a political objective; only joint security can guarantee personal security.

The classical philosopher Gorgias addressed this issue in his Olympian Speech:

> Men are aroused in the morning in war time by the trumpet and in peace by the crowing of cocks. . . . war very much resembles sickness and peace is very like health, for peace restores even the sick and in war even the healthy perish. In peace again we are told that the old are buried by the young as is natural, while in war it is the reverse, and that above all in war there is no safety even up to the walls, but in peace there is safety as far as the boundaries of the land.[1]

Modern-day terrorism proves how right Gorgias was: during wartime, security does not reach "even up to the walls." His words apply not only to urban terrorism (today a worldwide phenomenon) but also to missile attacks on the home front, not to mention missiles equipped with unconventional warheads. Thus, the difference between our world and ancient times is in the dimension of expected destruction. We can learn a great deal from the efforts that the superpowers and their allies have made to control the arms race, and it is not necessary that the first step toward an ultranational system or regional strategic defense pact be comprehensive or dramatic; progress can begin slowly.

In terms of territory, we can start in the Red Sea area. Over time, these shores have changed, and today Egypt, Sudan, and Eritrea line one side while Israel, Jordan, Saudi Arabia, and Yemen are on the other side. These countries have a common interest, and there are no grounds for conflict. Post-Mengistu Ethiopia and the newly independent Eritrea want to establish peaceful relations with their neighbors, including Israel. Egypt has already signed a peace treaty with Israel; and Jordan, Saudi Arabia, and Yemen want naval security and fishing and air rights. Initially, we can focus on human-interest issues, such as rescuing pilots and sailors, and on setting up a communications network to transmit early warnings of water or land maneuvers. The regional system can be maintained via joint projects—research, developing food sources from the sea, and tourism. A strategic pact will be possible only at a more advanced stage. With this as our ultimate goal, we can determine the interim steps.

People tend to remember more and think less. Our memories are familiar, affectionate, nostalgic. Our thoughts, which concentrate on the unfamiliar, are less welcoming. However, we must focus on this new Middle East reality, with its new dimensions and different nature of security, and not wander among memories of victories in long-gone wars—wars that will never be fought again.

6

FROM AN ECONOMY OF STRIFE TO AN ECONOMY OF PEACE

SINCE ISRAEL'S RECOGNITION IN 1948, ARAB countries have fought six wars with Israel (the War of Independence, the Sinai campaign, the Six-Day War, the War of Attrition, the Yom Kippur War, and the war with Lebanon) and another six among themselves (the war in Yemen, Black September in Jordan, the Lebanese civil war, the Iran-Iraq War, the conquest of Kuwait, and the Persian Gulf War). In addition, the region has seen numerable incidents of terrorism, which violated all political and moral rules of conduct, and a series of security actions and counteractions. These confrontations forced the various governments involved to earmark huge amounts of money and resources to

upgrade their armies and military infrastructures. Even in the in-
tervals between wars, Middle Eastern countries continued to participate in the ongoing arms race, working endlessly to modernize
their weapons systems and emphasizing military training and
buildup. These confrontations have sown only destruction and
devastation, ruined thousands of families, increased the level of
poverty, and ultimately led to the rise of fundamentalism, which
has further threatened national stability and created anarchy, but
has failed to solve any problems.

S O M E concrete figures provide a clear picture of the scope of
the problem:

Arms Race

On average, Middle Eastern countries invest a total of $60 billion
annually in arms purchases. During the Yom Kippur and Persian
Gulf wars, these figures reached unprecedented heights. Between
1973 and 1991, the Arab countries, and Iran in particular, pur-
chased $180 billion worth of weapons and other military equip-
ment. Since the 1991–92 Persian Gulf War, the Arab countries
and Iran have signed purchase orders with the United States,
Great Britain, France, China, and North Korea totaling $30
billion.

   This huge capital investment—or, rather, waste—was necessi-
tated by the technological revolution, which raised the price of
arms and precision weapons. An advanced fighter plane (an F-15
or Mirage 2000) costs about $60 million; an Apache missile, $20
million; a Patriot missile system, over $120 million; a Western-

made tank, $4 to $8 million; an Eastern-made tank, $1 million; a ground-to-ground C/B Scud missile, $1 million to $2 million, and a D ("no dong") Scud, $4 million to $6 million.[1] With an end to arms technology nowhere in sight, investments in this area are liable to skyrocket. Even should there be no wars for an entire decade, the countries will "need" to upgrade most of their weapons systems.

According to researchers, during the 1980s the Middle East was first in the world in arms and weapons outlays relative to gross national product. Figures show that investments in military equipment consumed 21 percent of all government budgets in the region (excluding defense aid, which is a central component of the Israeli and Egyptian budgets).[2] The Middle Eastern countries (including Iraq and Iran) spent an average of 17 percent of their gross domestic product (GDP) on defense. The largest outlays were made by Syria—almost 50 percent—followed by Israel, with 26 percent. (During the period surveyed, Israel fought the war in Lebanon, and the Israel Defense Forces retreated from Sinai and were redeployed in the Negev.) Kuwait spent the least—only 5 percent of its GDP went to military expenditures.[3]

The budget deficits and rising national debts of these Middle Eastern countries are direct results of this investment. In 1981, the region's overall national debt measured 35 percent of total exports; ten years later, it had reached 113 percent.[4]

Costs of Past Wars

The financial cost of the war in Lebanon to Israel alone was at least $4 billion.[5] This sum does not even approach the overall cost of the Persian Gulf War less than ten years later, which Arab sources estimate to be $676 billion,[6] not including the devastation to the Kuwaiti and Iraqi environments and lost economic growth in these and other Persian Gulf states.

Costs of Future Wars

Every day of total war would cost Israel at least $1 billion. This does not include massive damage to the country's physical infrastructure. The underlying assumption is that damage to the opponent will at least equal this estimate.

Investigations of weapons and tactics used in the Persian Gulf War illustrate that the battlefield of the future will be precise and limited. This will decrease damage to the surroundings, but will considerably increase damage to predetermined targets. Although we have no precise overall figures, reciprocal hits to the physical infrastructure will further increase the financial costs of war and will be affected by many factors. In any case, the cost will be greater than that in previous wars and may even exceed the overall damage caused by the Persian Gulf War. The terrible destruction will be pointless.

Indirect Costs

Besides direct costs, the ongoing conflict in the Middle East causes indirect damage to regional economics because of the absence of trade relations between neighboring countries, the large premiums that international insurance companies charge in high-risk areas, the loss of work days and investment owing to reserve duty (or alternatively, maintenance of a large permanent army), and underinvestment in economic development consequent to the channeling of all available funds into the arms race. The most serious by-product, however, is the exacerbation of poverty and distress. About 224 million people live in the Middle East and earn an average annual per capita income of $1,200. That is only one-tenth the average income in Europe, with a widening gap between oil-producing countries and the other countries of the region. The standard of living in the poorer countries of the Middle East is painfully low, while the birth rate is high and life expectancy is short. Table 1 (page 92) offers a general picture of the situation today.

These poor economic conditions are a breeding ground for fundamentalism. They encourage extremist demagogues who purport to speak in the name of God but who are incapable of solving the basic problems of human beings. Poverty is not a matter of chance, and hardship is not punishment from above. They are the product of human action. When we allocate so much money to increase a nation's destructive powers, too few resources are left to foster social and financial growth, creativity, and construction. Table 2 (page 93) illuminates the dynamics between investment in arms and investment in health and education.

MISERY and distress in the Middle East are products of the unending fear of an outbreak of yet another war, and not necessarily between Arabs and Israelis. Iran and Iraq, for example, spent enormous sums fighting one other, while solving none of their political, strategic, or economic problems. Thereafter, they were forced to revitalize their giant war machines. Iraq then invaded Kuwait and ultimately became embroiled in an all-out war against an international coalition led by the United States, with serious social and economic ramifications. Oman and Saudi Arabia target huge chunks of their budget for military needs, not because of a potential conflict with Israel but because of their very

Table 1

SOCIAL PROFILE OF THE MIDDLE EAST—1989

	Population (millions)	% Per Capita Income	Life Span	% Estimated Population Growth	% Illiterate Adults ('85)
Iran	53.3	2,530	63	3.3	49
Bahrain	0.5	6,380	69	2.8	81
Jordan	3.9	1,630	67	2.8	25
Israel	4.5	9,790	76	1.8	5
Kuwait	2.0	16,160	74	3.1	30
Lebanon	2.7	880	66	0.1	23
Libya	4.4	5,310	62	3.6	33
Egypt	51.0	640	60	1.8	39.4
Gulf Principalities	1.5	18,410	71	2.3	40
Syria	12.1	870	66	3.7	41
Saudi Arabia	14.4	6,020	64	3.7	49
Iraq	18.3	3,020	63	3.4	58.2
Oman	1.5	5,220	65	3.9	70
Yemen	11.7	600	52	3.6	80

Source: Stanley Fisher, "Prospects for Regional Integration in the Middle East," *paper presented at the World Bank Conference on Regional Integration, Washington, D.C., April 1–3, 1992.*

real fear of Iranian fundamentalism and Iraqi aggression. However, the Arab-Israeli conflict stands at the center of the Middle East arms race, justifies it ideologically, and sometimes lends it an almost ritualistic slant.

If war is the source of regional distress, the one and only solu-

Table 2

PUBLIC OUTLAYS FOR HEALTH, EDUCATION, AND DEFENSE (in percents)—1986

	Health	Education	Defense
Iran	1.4	5.5	20.0
Jordan	2.7	6.5	13.8
Israel	3.2	7.1	19.2
Kuwait	2.7	5.1	5.8
Libya	3.0	10.1	12.0
Egypt	1.1	5.4	8.9
Syria	0.4	2.9	14.7
Saudi Arabia	4.0	10.6	22.7
Iraq	0.8	3.7	32.0
Oman	2.3	5.3	27.6
Yemen	1.2	5.6	9.1
Mean, Middle East*	2.0	5.8	14.2
Mean, developing countries	1.4	3.7	5.5

Outstanding outlays by Iraq and Iran for defense (as a result of the war between them) were not included in the calculation of the regional mean.

Source: Human Development Report, 1991 *(published by the World Bank). Also, Stanley Fisher,* "Prospects for Regional Integration in the Middle East," *paper presented at the World Bank Conference on Regional Integration, Washington, D.C., April 1–3, 1992.*

tion is peace. In addition to the direct economic advantage of peace, a wide spectrum of fantastic opportunities will open up, with backing from local and foreign sources as well as government and international aid. It will take a generous infusion of capital to create a lasting peace. But not only will the investors and produc-

ers benefit, the consumers—the thousands who now live under
poor conditions—will gain. The continued advance toward economic compatibility among the countries of the region will enable
the ultimate establishment of a regional economic system aimed at
growth, development, and prosperity.

Experience has shown that a situation always turns out to be
more complicated than was expected in the planning stage. It is
inevitable that various difficulties will emerge in the transition
from a wartime to a peacetime economy, but they can be overcome. Indeed, they may even bolster fellowship among the nations of the region and speed the establishment of the regional
system. In other words, financial problems are the catalyst for
this regional economic system. If symbolic and emotional factors
delay the creation of such a body in the Middle East, we could use
international monies to establish a fund for Middle Eastern development, allowing every country that opens its borders to enjoy the
benefits. The funds could come from a joint European-American-
Japanese credit line, offered to help maintain the peace; from
income from the petroleum industry; from monies that remain
after lowering local investment in the arms race; and from savings
thanks to decreased military credit and aid.

Modern diplomacy is becoming increasingly involved in the
economic aspects of national and international policy. In the Middle East, this diplomacy has a moral mission with historic dimensions: to change the distorted relationship between investment in
military needs and investment in human needs; to decrease the
proportion of the national budget earmarked for waging war and
causing devastation; and to use public and international money
allocated for supporting the peace in order to further education,
democratization, and justice.

The post-World War II trend for countries to form economic
blocs has gained momentum with the recent decline of commu-

nism. For almost forty years, the European Common Market was limited territorially: it stopped where communism started. With the lifting of the Iron Curtain, Europe no longer has to fight a common enemy and no longer has to fear the spread of communism and oppressive rule. Although this also means that its primary motive for uniting is no longer valid, it has discovered a new challenge. Of course, meeting that challenge has proved very difficult, sometimes even more difficult than facing the enemy. When communism crumbled, Western Europe discovered 350 million new Europeans who embraced freedom but had no resources to finance it. They were educated, hungry, unemployed, and possessed nuclear weapons; and they appealed to Western European countries, whose borders were now open but whose gates were shut. To dispel the gathering political, social, and even security clouds, Western Europe realizes it must expand the Common Market to all countries on the continent. By the turn of the century, there will be a huge market—700 million to 800 million people—busy with its own undertakings, but with clear interests in other areas of the world, including the Middle East.

The United States is attempting to establish a free trade area with Canada and Mexico, and could possibly use the geographic proximity and organizational framework of the Americas to open a free trade area with Central America and parts of South America, including Brazil and Argentina. This common American market, which may be created before the end of the century, would likely comprise 1 billion people.

Even Asia shows signs of this trend toward regional unity. Thailand, Singapore, Sri Lanka, Indonesia, Taiwan, Vietnam, and South Korea—a group of countries with considerable economic weight—are starting to organize a common market. And China and India are huge markets in and of themselves.

Regional common markets reflect the new zeitgeist. As philos-

opher Georg Wilhelm Friedrich Hegel pointed out, statesmen are
not always aware of the spirit of the times when they make decisions, and only in retrospect does this spirit become obvious
within the sphere of universal history.[7] This regional view might
have been only a glimmer when the European Community began
to organize after World War II. Today its course is obvious, and
pushing onward.

With the establishment of these new world trade organizations, can the Middle East afford to remain on the sidelines? The
transition from an economy of strife to an economy of peace has
set the stage for the Middle East. We have a real interest in using
the peace opportunities at hand to raise the standard of living for
our region, our countries, and our citizens.

THE entire world has been wavering between the two poles that
emerged in the wake of the Enlightenment and the French
Revolution: unity and individuation. The desire for personal and
regional unity led to establishment of rational social frameworks,
while trends to nationalist and religious individuation gave life a
symbolic or spiritual basis. Even if we do not yet know which way
the scale of time is tipping and cannot assess the burgeoning spirit
of unity, we must not ignore this historic world movement. In the
not-too-distant past, history was a chain of military and political
conflicts; today, international relationships based on economics
are the dominant characteristic.

It is no coincidence that the trend toward regional economic
organization got under way in the second half of the twentieth
century. Tremendous investments in research and development
have became necessary to survive in a new world of open competition. Within a small economy, it is impossible to amass sufficient

funds to develop new products or to upgrade existing ones. Therefore, huge multinational corporations work alongside regional common markets in free trade areas to guarantee that all parties have a future in the modern world.

There is a connection between the emergence of these new regional organizations and the spread of democracy. In an economic democracy, goods are chosen much as are leaders in a political democracy—the best product wins. The market continuously demands new products that attract consumers. Competitive marketing is no less vital to an economy's growth than are production possibilities—and perhaps even more. Moreover, production potential depends on marketing potential; in order to justify such costly research and development, we need a consolidated marketing strategy to reach a gigantic consumer pool.

In a similar vein, modern marketing techniques are based on a rule borrowed from military strategists: concentrate on the opponent's weak point, and exploit breaks in defense and internal line movements. In the economic world, this means concentrating on consumers in a small area. Geographic proximity lends a relative edge, with the regional framework optimizing that advantage.

Even the face of international confrontation is changing, with the successful intelligence services of the cold war now collecting and studying economic and technological data. The world is being reorganized into a two-tiered economic structure: at the base are the regional communities, and above them stretch the international consortiums and worldwide organizations. This structure can already be seen in the political power these consortiums wield and the consequent development of international law, which will lead to diplomatic and legal recognition of the these giant groups. State sovereignty is limited today by international law, which requires each nation to behave according to rules acceptable to the

international community. At the same time, the world has begun
to recognize ultranational organizations as a political entity in
their own right. These include the United Nations and its branch
organizations, and regional organizations like the European Community, which also has a higher legal body directly elected by the
citizens of its member nations. So it can be seen that a new type of
citizenship is catching on, with a new personal identity, for Europeans as members of a European society. The "mother continent," on which most of the documented wars in history have
been conducted, stands at the threshold of a new international
reality based on peace and economic competition. In Western
Europe, particularist nationalism is fading and the idea of a "citi-
zen of the world" is taking hold. Nationalism has not disappeared,
of course, and its demise cannot yet be contemplated. However,
bloody wars such as that between Germany and France are a
thing of the past.

Like Eastern Europe, the Middle East has not yet enjoyed such
political and economic unity. Nevertheless, cooperation between
countries for their mutual benefit and for the good of their residents will also characterize the Middle East's economic transition
from confrontation to peace. Obviously, a readiness to base relationships on voluntary agreements between equal partners is a
prerequisite for this. Only economic relations that are a product
of free will, mutual respect, and true equality will yield fruit.

We can enter into this type of partnership immediately. Even
at the autonomy stage, Israel can form a real partnership with the
Palestinians, based on wisdom and fairness. We do not view the
agreement that was signed by us as a commercial one, but as a
historic commitment with an economic lining. This will be the
political significance of the passage from an economy of confrontation to an economy of peace, particularly at this most sensitive

juncture in the complex relationship between Arabs and Israelis. It will also enable us to jointly exploit our natural resources, to the advantage of both sides. In the words of the Palestinian economist Professor Hashem Aluartani from the Anaj'ah University in Nablus, "True recognition between sides, significant long-term differences in income and technological knowledge and essential differences in production costs—these are the factors that will contribute to the formation of economic cooperation. The two sides will also attain huge profits (or significant savings) if they refrain from unnecessary duplication of the capital infrastructure, and in the future Palestinians and Israelis will be able to develop joint economic internal and external enterprises."[8]

The next stage, after bilateral and multilateral relationships have been established, will entail formation of regional industries through the cooperation of international bodies and independent international consortiums. At this point, the regional economic process will be upgraded and the new reality, in which business precedes politics, will be instituted. Ultimately, the Middle East will unite in a common market—after we achieve peace. And the very existence of this common market will foster vital interests in maintaining the peace over the long term.

The Middle East will not always import unemployment and export hunger. A regional organization is inevitable here as well, where Western civilization began. The regional organization now dictates world policy, in which the market is more important than the individual countries, speed is more important than quantity, and a competitive atmosphere is more important than old borders.

7

Sources of Investment and Funding

A NEW MIDDLE EAST CANNOT BE ESTAB-
lished on a political basis alone. If we define change as erecting a
few new signs and marking off old borders, very little will have
been gained, and certainly none of it will last. The unrest will not
abate, because the reasons underlying it are more economic and
social than they are political. As long as the Middle East's food
supply is inadequate, and new food sources grow at a slower rate
than does the region's population, distress will continue—as will
its political expression, whether in the form of the black hoods of
revolutionaries or the white robes of religious fanatics.

Although Israel is increasingly aware of the benefit of modern economic power coupled with political and military power, many of its neighbors have not yet learned this lesson. The Palestinians have almost forgotten the economic aspect of their lives. The great majority of Arab leaders erred in assuming that honor could replace food. They are gradually losing public support, and their people are increasingly seeking answers in fundamentalist propaganda.

No, salvation will not come from "empty" political settlements that ignore the roots of anguish and distress. Some argue that, in addition to rampant poverty, disruptive fundamentalism gathers its strength from general opposition to modernization, which radical Muslim philosophy equates with the moral and cultural emptiness of Western democracy. Even if this is true, there is little chance of extinguishing this movement, with all its dangers, without engendering a basic change in Middle Eastern economics. The region must be given economic freedom—the sooner the better.

A modern economy is not an accident; it is born of hard work and creative thinking. Some of the basic rules for establishing a modern economy are clear: decrease the war chest; increase investment in education; use available natural reserves wisely and create alternatives as necessary; establish required energy and desalination plants; construct a state-of-the-art infrastructure for communications and transportation; develop industry, agriculture, and tourism, making use of all existing advantages; open borders and encourage competition.

As discussed in chapter 6, we must view the Middle East as a regional economic system so as to better cope with the grave tasks ahead of us. Nations cannot do it on their own. Organized into an economic entity, the region can develop markets that produce income instead of collect donations. Savings from decreased defense costs can refurbish obsolete bureaucratic systems, make better use of transportation, optimize land and natural reserves, and so on to benefit the economy.

To establish this new Middle East, we need large-scale, concentrated international investments. The regional system requires economic aid, in the broad sense of the term. Of course, the world does not lack countries that seek financial assistance. But the recent economic revival of countries that were in dire straits in the late seventies and early eighties has shown the effectiveness of such assistance. Their "new health" is proof of the worldwide benefit of foreign aid. This has been especially true for certain Asian and Latin American countries.

Few world leaders have envisioned the Middle East as a living economic organization. No one has mapped out the relative economic advantages of the region. Therefore, our first task is to gather and organize verifiable, up-to-date data for purposes of decision making. Up until now, Middle Eastern economics was anchored in two assumptions: defense costs are high and borders are closed. Peace, in and of itself, will alter these assumptions and open new opportunities.

T H E world economy currently revolves around three major markets: American, European, and Japanese. The United States is the most powerful country on the globe, and it has the inclination, assets, experience, confidence, and prestige to implement a high-quality international policy. As a superpower, the United States has been generous and supportive vis-à-vis military defense and economic rehabilitation. During the twentieth century, American soldiers twice crossed the ocean to fight on European soil, to help establish an international standard of freedom and justice. And it asked for nothing in return. The Marshall Plan after World War II

—intended to promote European postwar rehabilitation—was American born and bred. In addition, after World War II, the United States continued to maintain armed forces in Europe to combat the spread of communism. And when the Iron Curtain fell, Americans immediately offered economic aid to Mikhail Gorbachev, and later, to Boris Yeltsin, so that Russia could regain its footing and establish a market economy.

Likewise, America defeated Japan in World War II after a long and bitter campaign, then helped its recent enemy to make an astonishing economic recovery—in the hope that Japan could find an economic answer to the defeated despots. I believe that General Douglas MacArthur's greatest victory was not on the battlefield, but as allied commander of the Japanese occupation. He channeled his energy into constructive arenas, introducing a new lifestyle and economic model to the people of the Land of the Rising Sun. This enabled Japan to attain tremendous economic feats, which took the place of the military power it had lost.

The United States now faces economic difficulties of its own, and its ability to provide direct financial aid has significantly decreased. Although it continues to fulfill the mission imposed upon it—to be the largest builder of political bridges in history—it can no longer contribute as much financially to developing the lands on both sides of those bridges.

As for Europe, the tension between two main world historical trends—national unity and national individuation—is the backdrop for the economic development sweeping the continent. Although Europe presently is experiencing a drop in economic growth, it continues to be the largest market in the world, with 35 percent of the world's production and 45 percent of world trade.

Throughout history, Europe has been hesitant and overcautious, compared to the United States, with regard to investments in and aid to other nations. It took Europe a long time to free itself of its colonialist tradition, with its long habit of viewing colonies as a source of income, not as a target for investment. When Europe freed its holdings in Asia and Africa—or perhaps was freed of them—the status of some pivotal countries began to deteriorate—namely, Great Britain, Portugal, Holland, France, Germany, Belgium, Italy, and Spain. "Britannia," wrote Dean Acheson in *Present at the Creation,* "lost an empire but did not find a role."[1]

But Europe regained its world status after establishment of the Common Market, when the Mother Continent began to operate as a benevolent superpower. It established the European Investment Bank, which serves the needs of failing or underdeveloped European and non-European markets; it initiated (although within another framework) the establishment of a bank to assist Eastern Europe; and it directly contributed to areas where starvation was rampant and to aid desperate refugees. Even the Palestinians have received aid from Europe—in 1992, 90 million European Currency Units (ECUs) were earmarked for residents of the West Bank and the Gaza Strip. In addition, a few European countries have directly and very generously contributed up to 1 or 1.5 percent of their gross national product to help needy nations. At the close of the twentieth century, perhaps Europe has not yet equaled the United States in terms of economic aid, but it has definitely begun to follow in America's footsteps.

When Japan's program of postwar economic recovery began to show results, it behaved with understandable economic egotism. The only nation that had experienced the effects of nuclear weapons changed its orientation beyond recognition. In the first decades after the war, Japan needed a national policy that would define and establish a new self-image based on its ethnic and traditional values. Japan's shift from a position of military might was manifested in its national perspective: foreign policy was based on the assumption that the world revolves around economics, and everything—even the painful web of politics—ultimately is subservient to the balance sheet. Karl Marx would have been pleased, had not events produced some unexpected results.

Japan's bold capitalist venture eventually felt the effects of some nonmaterialistic principles governing world markets. The Japanese gradually realized that although their products were highly esteemed, their policies definitely were not; their goods became targets of worldwide animosity, endangering the country's continued prosperity. The Japanese understand that they must wrap their products not only in attractive packaging but also in benign politics. Therefore, they have begun to dramatically increase their budget for foreign aid. In light of the country's low defense costs relative to overall consumption—at most, 1 percent of Japan's GNP goes to defense, compared to 3 to 7 percent in other free-market countries—this sound economic power could invest even more capital abroad—if not to deter enemies, then to make friends.

An overview of today's world economy shows success in halting inflation, but that success is coupled with worrisome growth in unemployment. Masses of immigrants—the unemployed from underdeveloped nations—are knocking on the doors of their richer neighbors. In this new world order, people are free to cross national borders, but they are barred from enjoying its economic benefits. Far better if these people, who represent a huge potential market, received help to develop their own countries.

From this we can see that Europe and Japan, which are growing rapidly economically, can take an example from the United States and help rehabilitate the underdeveloped areas of the world, including the Middle East. In the long run, it is in the interests of the entire world to help the Middle East become a viable economic entity.

THE components of a wide-ranging financial plan to rehabilitate this region will involve the multiple institutions of the developed world. These embrace four spheres of activity: political, managerial, financial (banking), and operational.

Political Sphere

In Europe, decisions involve the Council of Ministers, with members from the twelve countries that make up the European Community. In the United States, there must be agreement between the executive branch of the federal government and Congress. In Japan, decisions are linked between the central government and commercial interests.

Managerial Sphere

In Europe, the managerial aspect pertains to the operative institutions of the Common Market; in the United States, responsibilities are distributed among the various levels of government. Japan's unique decision-making process is based more on growing consensus than on a determined hierarchy.

Financial (Banking) Sphere

In all three major world markets, national and international banking systems control the collection and distribution of funds. Banks today also fund new (or additional) areas of activity.

Operational Sphere

In all three regions, large national or multinational corporations control the elements of production and marketing. Today, markets are becoming almost more important than politics.

A new, peaceful Middle East will be welcomed and supported by leading political figures and commercial organizations. Along with their desire to save this sensitive area from hunger and the ravages of war, these three financially stable regions of the world are showing increased interest in developing the Middle East's trade and transportation routes. They aim to instill a harmonious environment here, as a bulwark against nuclear weapons and the terror and violence of religious radicalism. These are the two main threats to the world's petroleum market—the lifeblood of modern economics—which, like the human circulatory system, requires stability and equilibrium.

Indeed, the developed nations of the world have great political and economic interest in the Middle East. America invests the lion's share of its foreign aid here, and is a leader in the peace process. And although it is too early to judge the size of this as yet unestablished regional market, the potential of the Middle East economic region cannot be ignored.

In our relationship with Europe, the economic benefits are not only theoretical. The European Community has long had interest in the Middle East, with Common Market institutions bound by agreements and close relations with a number of Middle Eastern countries. The European Community has proposed the creation of a Mushraq market parallel to the Maghreb market, with which they have special relations. The Mushraq consists of six parties—Egypt, Syria, Jordan, Lebanon, Israel, and the Palestinians—whereas the Maghreb comprises three countries—Morocco,

Tunisia, and Algeria. According to this idea, there should be an interlinkage between the three markets.

Europe is also a major player in the multilateral negotiations (determined by the Madrid Conference)—talks that are designed to lay the groundwork for a new Middle East. The countries of Europe are active in all five working groups—economics, ecology (environmental protection), arms control, refugee management, and water. The groups will create new visions for the Middle East and strategies for their implementation.

Japan is also showing increasing interest in the Middle East negotiations, and has taken a leading role in developing tourism possibilities and environmental protection.

Unfortunately, political accords and government decisions are not enough. Success is dependent greatly on the responsiveness of private companies—American, European, and Asian, and now Middle Eastern as well. Already, there have been intriguing attempts to establish Middle Eastern companies, using American, European, Asian, Arab, and Israeli capital. This type of partnership investment is expected to yield both optimum economic profit and political benefit.

I HAVE had some interesting discussions with European leaders and with senior managers of leading corporations. They have reacted positively to the idea of participating in the establishment of an economic infrastructure in the new Middle East. During his visit to Israel, President François Mitterrand and I had long conversations on Middle Eastern economics. He promised that France would propose that the European Investment Bank set aside about 1 billion ECU to establish regional industries in such areas such as transportation and desalination.

I had a similar conversation with Chancellor Helmut Kohl of

Germany. He agreed that the economic problems in his now-unified country were largely a product of West German success prior to unification, rather than the result of East Germany's failure. Productivity rose to the point that it began to generate unemployment. In response, West Germany cut its work week and lengthened yearly vacations, but to no avail. Improvements in working conditions added work-hours to the German economy, but could not halt the growth in unemployment.

I suggested to the Chancellor that a possible way to reduce German unemployment might be new sources of business, even novel ones like developing new markets in the Middle East. Chancellor Kohl showed great interest in the idea. I added that market growth today is a function not only of the number of consumers but also the level of consumption. Raising people's standard of living is preferable to maintaining an existing standard of living. Countries with high per capita income will buy more and thereby meet their debts to foreign banks. Chancellor Kohl and I discussed the example of U.S. aid for Russian immigrant absorption in Europe. Former President Bush had put up $10 billion in loan guarantees for building an economic infrastructure, with money set aside against default. If Europe follows the same route, providing similar guarantees to European companies investing in the Middle East, Europe will help solve its own problems while also helping the new Middle East.

I also spoke with Jacques Delors, President of the EC Commission. He was particularly interested in three areas: establishing a power station, building desalination plants, and fighting the war against desertification. He asked his assistants to prepare detailed plans for cooperative actions.

United States Secretary of State Warren Christopher told me on his own initiative that American companies must assume a large proportion of this giant task. The State Department invited about fifty heads of large American corporations to detail the development needs of the Middle East and suggest the hidden opportunities that lay there.

A few large corporations have already begun work. For example, one of the largest and best-known companies in Europe is investigating the possibility of setting up a company to manufacture trucks, based partly in Egypt, partly in Jordan, and partly in Israel. The trucks would be produced by all three countries, and a market would be created in all three.

The world has more money than ideas. The new Middle East is an idea whose time has come. The world's major corporations can help our dream come true, and by helping us they will also help themselves.

THERE is no doubt that it would be possible to get assistance from existing sources, such as the World Bank, the European Investment Bank, and private banks. I believe, however, it is preferable to concentrate all investment money for Middle Eastern development in a bank set up exclusively for that purpose. This approach offers a number of important advantages. First, only 1 percent of the necessary capital is needed to establish the bank. Second, from a sociopsychological standpoint, the bank will encourage people living in the Middle East to see the regional framework as an entity in its own right. Every child knows the concept of a bank; Israelis often say "Better banks than tanks." This regional bank will attract new investors, and collect funds from the region itself.

Some experts have suggested working through the World Bank. However, the World Bank is not the optimal vehicle under existing conditions in the Middle East. First, the Palestinians do not belong to it. Second, it is a cumbersome, slow-working body and it will take years before we see any aid. Lastly, Egypt could not enjoy any benefits because of its outstanding debts, and Israel is not included in the countries entitled to its aid. Yet if the World Bank will adapt itself to the urgent needs—and its management is showing a readiness to do so—it can become an early instrument in the development of interim-Palestinian self-government and the development of the region.

Therefore, it seems that Israel, together with Jordan, the Palestinians, and Egypt—the main partners for peace—must soon establish our own financial organ. It can be set up under the aegis of the World Bank, but it will be separate from it organizationally. The bank should be able to deal quickly and effectively with our new needs. It will be located in the Middle East, and be run by local people, who will have to make do with lower salaries and poorer conditions than are standard for richer international institutions.

SUPPORT from countries outside the region should take two forms: several hundred million dollars in capital, and guarantees on corporate bonds sold in the international money market. The regional bank will investigate the merits of specific projects and will support those approved at lower than market value. The operating costs of the bank will be financed by profits and the proceeds from capital investments. Bank policy will give clear preference to projects that require regional cooperation, such as communications networks, agriculture, water supply, energy production, and transportation.

Capital can be divided into three categories. First, funds will be collected from the region itself. The peace accords must set supplemental agreements that cut arms costs by one-third or even by one-half. That will release $20 billion for investment in regional peace. Perhaps the time has come for the oil-producing countries to contribute 1 percent of their income to regional development. This will have almost no effect on the price of oil, yet will help free these countries from threats to government stability. By opening borders and developing tourism, we can amass investment capital for trade, transportation, and tourist services.

Second, large international corporations will contribute capital via private investment. Developing the physical infrastructure—transportation, communications, and natural resources (especially desalination)—will generate orders for equipment and create jobs. Long-term credit must be extended under reasonable conditions, backed by government guarantees or by the participating common markets. In this manner, companies will get lucrative contracts, utilize their surplus production resources, and participate in this new opportunity for a promising investment.

Third, direct aid can be channeled to distressed populations, such as in the Gaza Strip, by using some of the foreign financial resources earmarked for humanitarian purposes.

Every investment in the Middle East will prove itself and yield a return, whether in the form of stable oil prices or through a savings in military expenditures. The new Middle East, economically developed and socially and politically stable, will cost the world far less than would a violent political confrontation, in which other nations would have to intervene. Therefore, our large international and regional mission meshes with contemporary opportunity, if only we can recognize this historic time.

8

THE GREEN
BELT

THE PROTRACTED CONFLICT IN THE MIDDLE
East affected all nations in the region, including the outlook of
their leadership. Arabs and Israelis became embroiled in the politics and strategies of confrontation: the threat of a future war
overshadowed all other considerations. Yet while they guard the
areas under their sovereignty, Arab leaders are gradually losing
their fertile land. And this time, they are surrendering without a
fight.

The enemy today is the desert. The desert is taking over more
and more of the fertile land on which we all depend. The Arab
world controls a considerable portion of the earth—13 million

square kilometers—but 89 percent of this immense area is already desert. If we stand idle, another quarter of the remaining 11 percent will be lost by the end of the decade.

DESERTIFICATION is a problem worldwide, and the United Nations and many countries are involved in trying to control it. Desertification is the result of several processes related in outcome, but different in nature. The first—natural expansion— occurs along the periphery of the desert; it is not a man-made phenomenon, but we can help stop it. The second process—land degradation—is the direct result of human exploitation and neglect. It occurs on arid and semiarid land, not necessarily border areas, and may even be a problem in regions with relatively high annual rainfall—up to sixty inches.

In addition to extreme weather conditions and a lack of water, according to research conducted by the United Nations, the main ecological factor in desertification is overuse of natural resources for maximum economic gain. When we ignore the needs of the environment, the land is depleted and its inhabitants are forced to move to other, less desirable areas. The land left behind is further neglected, resulting in underuse of its remaining resources. The latter stems from three factors: rapid population growth, impoverishment of farmers, and defective national planning.

Population growth is the main factor contributing to the overuse of natural resources. As population grows, land productivity falls. Overuse of water resources leads to greater salinity of both land and groundwater, while overuse of pastureland ruins its future potential. In this way, we upset the balance of a sensitive ecosystem and allow destructive natural phenomena to take over. The desertification process passes the point of no return: heat, drought, shifting sands, and lack of fertilization turn arable land into barren wasteland. When the land produces insufficient food, the result is poverty—the product of uncontrolled population growth and desert encroachment.

Desertification is threatening the people and environment of the Middle East. The desert may well swallow up the once-rich Fertile Crescent. It is imperative that the Middle East amass its resources to check the spread of the desert—the enemy of the entire region. Our energies must focus on this front, and victory will depend on our use of two basic tools: water and science.

WATER is not a product of politics, it is a product of nature. It flows underground and meanders about, ignoring maps and borders. Rain does not pass through customs checks, and streams do not need visas. Nevertheless, the water shortage has been growing more acute for generations. In Egypt, for example, the population has grown tenfold in the twentieth century, but the Nile has actually lost some of its good water. As it passes from its source in central Africa to the delta at the Mediterranean, it must supply all the thirsty people—and not only Egyptians—who live along its shores. Their misuse of its waters for improper irrigation decreases the amount available to everyone else. Other factors include growing urbanization and modernization. Not only has the population grown, but so has the relative water requirement per person, so that water demand is ten times higher today than it was a century ago. To put it bluntly, things are steadily getting worse.

As with other problems, the solution lies in reason and understanding. Setting priorities for water use is a basic element of economic policy in many parts of the world. Water usage will be a central political issue in the Middle East as well. Since the water shortage is far more serious than the lack of land, we must recycle water, we must produce water via desalination; and we must develop new types of food that require less irrigation. We must, and we can.

We can achieve these aims using modern technology, which finds practical applications for scientific findings ranging from computer-controlled irrigation to food production in vivariums to desalination. When Russia renewed diplomatic relations with Israel in 1991, among the first things the Russians did was buy cows from us. It came out that an Israeli cow provides three times more milk than a Russian cow. Actually, it is the same cow, with the same horns; the difference is in the system—scientific and technological—that we have applied to our stables. One can say, almost laughingly, that a modern system produces more milk than nature's cow.

Technological knowledge has also opened up new fields such as marine biology. Throughout history, people have fished from the sea to provide food. Until now, pisciculturists have bred fish and other marine animals in relatively small bodies of water. To prepare for the future, however, scientists are seeking ways to use the sea as a laboratory, so that we may replace or supplement that which nature has made available. Likewise, regions with more precipitation are showing mounting interest in exploiting scientific knowledge to develop new foods and new ways of producing food, largely as a response to environmental pollution.

These and other exciting developments will increase our ability in the Middle East to cope with difficult environmental conditions to halt the desertification process and increase our food supply.

AT the threshold of our new era is perhaps the greatest scientific promise: the brand-new field of biotechnology. Even under difficult climatic conditions, biotechnology can help us produce more fruits and vegetables, meat and fish, eggs and milk products, oils and beverages, in addition to spices, flowers, and perfumes. Biotechnology will revolutionize our methods of cultivation and irrigation, with a consequent boom in yield.

Although agriculture will always remain a cooperative venture between people and nature, and will always be affected by natural factors and human skill, it is rapidly becoming part of the technological sciences. It won't be long before the "power of technology," in the words of historian Paul Kennedy, will answer the needs of the "power of the population."[1] World population is expected to reach 10 billion by the year 2050. This fact is already presenting unprecedented challenges to scientists and statesmen alike. We cannot wait indefinitely to realize the true potential for progress, prosperity, and peace when we channel our creative energies, intelligence, and material resources into applied science and technology. We have reached the moon, but we have not overcome indigence and need; millions still die of starvation. Particularly in underdeveloped countries, the population is growing at a rapid rate, while the law of diminishing returns is applicable to agriculture. Thomas Malthus posited that an increase in population relative to an increase in the means of subsistence, unless controlled, would lead to poverty and war, which would serve as a "natural" restriction on growth of the population. Biotechnology would seem to put an end to this pessimistic scenario.

We have not yet found a way to employ genetic theory to raise sufficient quantities of plants and animals, and further research is necessary. But in this post–cold war era, we have the opportunity to change our perspective in applying scientific achievements. Governments are obligated now to allocate the necessary resources to exploit biotechnological potential in agriculture, health, and environmental protection. For sure, this will be the key to growth and progress for everyone.

ISRAEL has a relative advantage in using basic and applied research for agriculture and desertification. It increased its agricultural yield by twelve times in twenty-five years—from 1950 to 1975—virtually without increasing the size of the arable land. The estimate is that 95 percent of the increase was the result of science, technology, and planning. It is ready to place its knowledge at the disposal of its neighbors, not out of altruism but because we all live in this region and are obligated to help each other overcome the difficulties imposed by nature. We need not wait until peace is officially established to start our technological partnership. We are already conducting cooperative ventures with friendly countries that have full diplomatic relations with Israel, such as Egypt; this is also true for a number of countries that have not yet established full diplomatic relations with us, such as Morocco. Thanks to King Hassan, Morocco is already enjoying agricultural cooperation through research and development institutes in the United States and Israel.

Of the projects now being planned in Israel, several focus on intensive desert agriculture, aimed at increasing productivity by applying the scientific knowledge accumulated during development of the Negev Desert and Arava Depression. At the same time, we must develop integrative settlements in the desert and on its periphery to replace the animal life that currently contributes to desertification, and we must breed sheep and cattle that are more suitable for desert conditions. When Syria is ready to do so, it will particularly benefit from joint projects in these areas.

The research and development should be organized on a multilateral basis, using three research centers—one in Israel, one in the United States, and one in an Arab country, as determined by the relevant academic bodies. All projects will be coordinated by one umbrella organization, which would probably be composed of members from Mediterranean countries that suffer the agricultural problems of arid regions. These include Morocco, Tunisia, Egypt, Israel, Syria, Turkey, Cyprus, and Spain. The main research topics would be agricultural methods for arid and semiarid regions; development of water sources and methods for using them; and rehabilitation of land and environmental systems that deteriorated as a result of desertification. This proposal has already received approval from important members of the international community, including President François Mitterrand of France, Vice-President Al Gore of the United States, and official representatives of Egypt, Tunisia, Morocco, Cyprus, Turkey, Japan, the United Nations, and the World Bank.

THUS, the Middle East can change color from brown to green. Success depends as much on us as it does on nature or the hand of God. If we continue to exploit the land without considering its needs, if we continue to dry it out and salinate it, we will have bequeathed hunger, want, and destitution to future generations. Instead we must establish a headquarters for the war against the desert, for the wise use of water, for agricultural research and development. This historic task will be to encircle our torrid region with a belt of green so that it will not lose its productivity and not turn into a human and economic wasteland. When the Middle East regional system becomes a reality, this research center will be accorded an honorable place in the world's scientific community. There is no need to delay its establishment until we complete the many political procedures for peace; drought does not wait, and encroachment by the desert does not cease. We must not waste precious time.

International sources of financial aid are already showing interest in our green belt. Within the framework of the multilateral negotiations, the World Bank has proposed encouraging cooperative technology and desert control operations in the Middle East. This initiative signaled recognition of the urgent need for cooperation in the region. Every country has achieved certain technological advances, and each has had its unique experience. Some projects have already been attempted, and others are in the pilot stage. Pooling our technology is the solution, though any tense situation in the region prevents full cooperation.[2] Even if the first attempts are "baby steps," they can be the basis for true coordinated action among countries of the region, with the help of world institutions, umbrella organizations, and other sources.

TO paint the Middle East green is the way to guarantee sufficient food, clean air, and an equitable environment free of fear and oppression. No one is placing an embargo on scientific and technological data for the fight against the desert. We can do it. We have to remove the desert from the land, the salt from the water, and the violence from the people. We can and we must.

9

THE LIVING
WATERS

A JEWISH SAYING GOES AS FOLLOWS: ALL
the miracles that God granted the people of Israel were involved
with water. Water is scarce in our torrid region of the world. Even
in biblical times, people sought ingenious ways to transport and
store water. They developed a system of canals and aqueducts to
move water from the rivers and streams to the cities, and they
used cisterns to collect the occasional rainwater. Some of the
world's first uses of water power were in Egypt and the Fertile
Crescent, and later in Israel, in an attempt to optimize water use.[1]

The region's water shortage had a strong impact on Islamic
architecture, and contributed to the Muslim practice of placing

many large-roomed, cool buildings around a large central court-
yard that held the wells.[2] Water is an essential part of Jewish,
Christian, and Moslem rituals, such as washing of the hands
(Jews), baptism (Christians), and washing of the feet (Muslims).

Since the dawn of history, there have been disputes, even wars,
over the ownership and use of water, and their outcome has
greatly affected regional order. No wonder water was afforded a
prominent place in ancient Middle Eastern cultures. It continues
to be a key consideration in modern political policy. Relationships
among the countries of the region were, and continue to be, dictated largely by water policy. Just as shepherds in biblical times
were concerned about differences over water, today a serious
violation of water rights is sometimes recognized as justification
for war.

THERE are four main reasons for the region's lack of water
today: natural phenomena, rapid population growth, heedless exploitation of the environment, and misguided policy. Nature does
not bless the Middle East with an abundance of freshwater. Precipitation is low compared with nearby Europe, droughts are fre-
quent, and there are few rivers. A number of scientists predict
that droughts will increase in the near future.[3] The Volga and the
Dnieper, the Danube and the Rhine, not to mention the Missis-
sippi and the Amazon, are far not only geographically but also
symbolically. Neither the Nile River—the longest in the world—
nor the Tigris and Euphrates—the life-sustaining arteries of the
Middle East—can fulfill the ever-growing needs of the region.
And this is even truer for the smaller rivers, such as the Orontes,
Jordan, Yarmuk, or Litani. Thus, the Middle East always lacks
water because of a relative paucity of natural sources.

These natural factors are exacerbated by the sins of people. The population explosion is the prime culprit. Rapid growth in population is not matched with a concomitant growth in food production, so poverty is worsening. Available water shrinks each year, and the quality of that water is compromised from overuse that results in salination and desertification. All these factors have an adverse affect on public health and lower the standard of living. Thus, we get sucked into a vicious cycle: the worse the poverty, the more the population grows, the worse the water shortage becomes, the worse the poverty gets, the more the population grows. Government steps to save water and properly utilize the existing water supply are at best of only marginal benefit.

The only way to break the cycle is to change basic cultural values and build a new economic infrastructure. And this type of change can be effected only by rapid modernization and democratization—processes that stress women's rights and parental authority, and that place responsibility for the fate of our children on us, not only on the Almighty. A few areas are showing signs of change, but they are only the very beginning.

EGYPT'S water problem is especially serious. The Aswan High Dam, built in the fifties, was intended to guarantee a regular, ample water supply even in times of drought. But the water level is steadily declining because of an extended drought in Ethiopia, coupled with evaporation and seepage. The arable land—already limited by the desert climate—is becoming sparse at a time when the population is rapidly increasing. By the end of the century, Egypt's population will reach 70 million. There is an immediate need to stem this looming Malthusian threat. We must facilitate development of an industrial, transportation, and tourism infrastructure and move toward mechanized agriculture. At the same time, there may be a need for international development projects to improve the Nile's water supply and to introduce conservation methods in the three countries most severely affected: Egypt, Sudan, and Ethiopia.

Syria, too, has more people than it can properly feed. Like Egypt, Syria once had enough food to export, but as a result of rapid population growth, it has been forced to become an importer. Syria is the weakest side of the triangle formed with Turkey and Iraq in the Tigris and Euphrates basin. With the dissolution of the Soviet Union, previously Damascus's primary source of financial support, Syria has been cut off from the West. Even Syrian participation in the 1991 coalition against Saddam Hussein did not catapult Syria into the western world. Successive years of drought in the region, and decreased water flow in the Tigris caused by Turkey's development projects, has exposed President Hafiz al-Assad's water policy, which proposes new dams, including one to divert the Tigris. The latter could rekindle tensions with Iraq: Iraq is concerned that it will be impossible to run a hydroelectric power station on the dwindling Tigris River, a situation that will lead to electricity shortages.[4]

The forecast for population growth in Syria for the year 2000 illustrates how much the trend is worsening. Within only ten years, Syria's population will increase from 12.6 million to 18.0 million, a growth of 50 percent. Population growth in Iraq is slightly lower because of the many wars that country has fought in recent years: from 18.8 million in 1990 to an expected 26.0 million by 2000. In the wake of a modernization and democratization campaign in Turkey, the growth rate of that country's population has slowed considerably. Of the three countries, Turkey is the only one in which food production rose by a higher percentage than did the population.[5]

Our environment is being destroyed as a result of population growth and consequent overuse and depletion of water sources. According to research conducted by Professor Arnon Sofer of the University of Haifa, the countries of the region have been overtaken by a "mania for developing projects for full-scale exploitation of the river and stream waters."[6] Their sole objective is to increase food production. Therefore, many dams are being built, ignoring the rights and needs of neighboring countries and having a negative impact on water quality. Moreover, too much groundwater is being drawn out from land along the Israeli, Syrian, Egyptian, and Libyan coasts, and the wells are in danger of saltwater intrusion. The tragedy is that overdevelopment, which also entails the risk of military confrontation, cannot solve the problem and will likely aggravate it.

THE fourth cause of the water shortage is misguided policy. National water policies are inconsiderate of the needs of neighboring countries and future generations. This attitude can drag countries back to the threshold of war. Sometimes the issue takes on unexpectedly large dimensions; this was the case in the crisis between Israel and Syria when Syria attempted to redirect the Jordan away from Israel's National Water Carrier. The situation gained momentum when the Soviets intervened, and the issue became more serious than Syria had anticipated. It eventually evolved into the preparations that led to the Six-Day War.

The water shortage exacerbates not only the Arab-Israeli conflict but also the civil war in Sudan and tensions between the radical Sudanese government and the moderate Egyptian one. Serenity and stability are not foreseeable in the Nile Delta, the Fertile Crescent, or the Orontes basin. And if Israel does not make peace with Syria, Lebanon, and Jordan, the Jordan and the Yarmuk basins may again become sources of dangerous hostility.

Like all wars in the political and strategic reality of our times, wars fought over water do not solve anything. Gunfire will not drill wells to irrigate the thirsty land, and after the dust of war has settled, the original problems remain. No war can change geographical givens: the desert covers about 60 percent of Israel, 70 percent of Syria, 85 percent of Jordan, and 90 percent of Egypt. The water shortage, therefore, requires a basic change in policy among the countries of the region. If no solution is found, our children will find it impossible to live here. How can we prepare them for the future?

In line with Jean-Jacques Rousseau, we might say that water does not "belong" to any one person or one country, but to humankind.[7] The water in the Middle East belongs to the region and its peripheral areas. More than any other issue, the water shortage proves the objective necessity of establishing a regional system. Only with this system can we all plan and administer water development projects and allocate water on an economic basis, in an honest and equitable manner.

This need to establish a regional water policy has arisen because the water shortage is worsening and the doctrine governing water rights does not discuss the absolute sovereignty of each nation over drainage from the basin within its domain. A cooperative regional body with participation by all affected countries will do much to ensure more equitable planning and allocation, will ease conflicts, and will work toward peace. The regional system goes beyond particularist nationalism to work for the overall interests of all inhabitants of the region. Unlike a network of separate nations, a regional system will not need an intermediary to match human needs with those of the various countries involved. Rather, through its activities it will create a lasting partnership among the region's countries, based on real interests.

THERE is no reason to wait to establish a regional water system. The bilateral and multilateral settlements and agreements provide a series of measures in two main areas: transfer of water from areas of plenty to areas of need; and desalination.

Water can be moved either directly, using an open canal or pipeline, or indirectly via containers. The first method is accepted practice in a number of Middle Eastern countries, and is the basic engineering principle employed by the National Water Carrier in Israel, and in canal systems used since antiquity in Egypt and Iraq. Each of these systems operates within one country, and that country draws the water from sources within its borders and transfers and allocates the water as it sees fit. But this is not enough. Most countries in the region do not have an abundance of water, and the best sources are always located outside the boundaries of countries that need it most. A better answer would be an international pipeline to bring water from country to country. Pipelines for water, oil, and gas should be laid out with an economic rationale and not based on the old strategic worries.

This idea is not new. In 1987, at the Center for Strategic and International Studies in Washington, D.C., Turkey proposed building a conduit, or "peace pipe," to carry excess water from its wetter regions to Middle Eastern countries with a water shortage.[8] The original plan involved two main conduits, one eastern and one western, that would eventually have secondary branches. The eastern conduit would extend through Syria to Jordan and Saudi Arabia, and from there to the Gulf principalities and Oman. The western line would bring water to Syria, Israel, the West Bank, and Jordan, and from there to Saudi Arabia. The Arab nations, however, refused to include Israel in the plan, arguing that this was not feasible because the Israeli-Palestinian conflict—which had certain hydrological implications—had not been settled. Turkey, therefore, decided to start with the eastern conduit, and this project is still far from the completion stage.

If the absence of peace between Israel and its neighbors, especially the Palestinians, is what held up the western conduit, then progress in the peace process also should mean progress in the water project, should it prove economically viable. Feasibility depends on the relative price of this water versus desalinated water and on encouragement from nations outside the region, who might see the project as a stabilizing force to safeguard other important interests as well. In addition to the project's geopolitical advantages to Turkey, the conduit might help stabilize the regional system, benefiting the oil-producing countries and their many clients. The major drawback is the long time required for completion. It will take at least ten years, perhaps even twenty, to meet the region's demand for water. Until then, we must find an alternative, because we cannot live with the status quo for another ten to twenty years. Therefore, although the conduit project is a valid option to increase the water supply and bolster pre-peace interests, we must also seek other faster and simpler solutions.

One such possible solution is giant containers. Again, Turkey appears to be the best source for the water, because any other country will be too far from the region, raising transportation costs and making the endeavor economically unfeasible. The water could be transported overland (via an elaborate railway network) or by sea (in tankers or in a convoy of relatively light Medusa containers on appropriate vessels). It is also possible, of course, to design an integrated system of water and land transport, in addition to local pipelines, similar to the Iran-Israel oil pipeline that operated until the rise of Khomeinism. However, since the main consideration is economic, this option might be more expensive than desalination. On the other hand, the project would involve a number of countries, creating a system of lasting relationships and mutual interests. The resulting peace conditions may, in turn, lower the price of water.

To better understand possibilities at hand, consider the example of transporting water in Medusa containers from southern Turkey to a port to be built in the Gaza Strip. From the Gaza Strip, the water would travel via conduit to Jordan, Saudi Arabia, and the Negev in Israel. We could thereby guarantee a regular water supply to at least four consumer partners in arid regions and create a common, concrete interest in maintaining peace. The time needed to build this apparatus is no greater than that needed to implement Turkey's "peace pipe," and it would offer the option of expanding the larger system, especially the eastern conduit. Planning and building an integrated system would open up employment opportunities in Europe, and the subsequent Middle East stability would have a positive effect on European economic interests.

THESE ideas introduce the possibility of further research and development in desalination. The Middle East is a pioneer in this area on a global scale: at the end of the previous decade, close to 5 billion cubic millimeters of water were desalinated annually worldwide, with half in the Middle East, especially in Saudi Arabia, Kuwait, and the Gulf principalities. Eilat and Aqaba have desalination facilities to meet the needs of their residents. The oil-producing countries can desalinate water on a large scale; they have no freshwater sources, and for them the oil required for desalination is cheaper than water. Therefore, desalination in some Middle Eastern areas is economically viable, but this is not yet true in Israel, Jordan, Syria, and Egypt.

We are not talking only of the economic side of desalination. The sum total of desalinated water worldwide is equal to the water Egypt consumes in one month, or the water needed to balance its expected yearly deficit of water by the end of the century. Is it technologically possible to raise the output of desalination plants while lowering their operating costs? Making desalination a practicable alternative would require a break-through; we do not as yet have the answer. One option is to integrate the desalination installations with the canal's hydroelec-tric system.[9] This would help Israel and Jordan overcome many difficulties, including desalination. But progress on a regional scale necessitates integrating all methods, continuing with existing research projects, and establishing new research institutes, run jointly by the countries of the region and outside parties.

IN addition to these considerations, we must weigh the possibil-ity of earmarking for technological development some of the money saved by establishing peace. The water that will irrigate the fields of the Middle East and quench the thirst of its people will help produce the fruits of peace. In the words of the prophet Isaiah: "I will open rivers on high places and fountains in the midst of the valleys; I will make the wilderness a pool of water, and the dry land springs of water. I will plant in the wilderness the cedar, the acacia tree, and the myrtle, and the oil tree; I will set in the Arava cypress, maple and box tree together" (Isaiah 41:18–19). If roads lead to civilization, then water leads to peace.

10

THE TRANSPORTATION AND COMMUNICATIONS INFRASTRUCTURE

FOR THE MIDDLE EAST, THE TRANSITION from an economy of strife to an economy of peace will mean channeling resources to develop an infrastructure appropriate for this new era of peace. This implies, of course, building support structures in all parts of all countries in the region. Although any effort made toward economic and social advancement is beneficial, special value is accorded to the development of a physical infrastructure close to sensitive national borders.

After withdrawing its forces from the Sinai after the 1973 Yom Kippur War, Egypt upgraded its navigational facilities in the Suez Canal, rehabilitated the canal cities, and improved access to those cities. Israel interpreted this development as a sign that Egypt had moved away from a strategy of hostility. In retrospect, the policy did indeed reflect the historic changes that President Sadat would later implement. He made the first steps a few years before his 1977 visit to Jerusalem: Egypt's development of the border areas, which had shortly before been a battlefield, were an appropriate beginning for this breakthrough. President Hosni Mubarak has kept up the momentum. Cairo and Alexandria have changed beyond recognition: high bridges and wide streets, built under the personal supervision of the President, now crisscross these two large cities. President Mubarak is likely to go down in history as one of the great builders of Egypt. Leaders who build bridges between cities are often those who build bridges between nations.

As Egypt has proved, there is no reason to wait for completion of the peace process to build a physical infrastructure. Development can—and must—precede the diplomacy, accelerating the entire process. Israel has already begun to move in this direction, and the government elected in July 1992 is making every effort to funnel resources into building roads and railroads, installing communications lines, and so on, rather than establishing new settlements—in contrast to the policy of the Likud government. Jordan, too, is showing a positive attitude toward physical development. The Palestinians are planning to undertake similar projects under self-rule, and we hope that Syria and Lebanon will take their cue from them.

Building roads, laying railway lines, marking off air routes, connecting transmission networks, advancing avenues of communication, making oil and water available everywhere (according to economics, not politics), and computerizing production of goods and services will breathe new life into the Middle East, just as the blood coursing through our veins distributes the oxygen necessary for life.

Even one-sided development geared to peace is welcome. But large-scale projects require international cooperation that advance and upgrade the peace process even more. This cooperation will take place on three levels. At the ground level, we will discuss how to settle the conflicting needs and interests of neighboring countries (for example, not conducting military exercises near the neighbor's tourist attractions). On the intermediate level, we will talk about how to adapt the infrastructure of all countries to certain engineering and technical specifications and to the economic conditions of participating and neighboring countries (for example, planning national roads and railroads to allow future linkup and greater development of transportation lines).

The first two levels are designed to ensure good relations with adjacent countries. At the top level of talks, countries will discuss working toward complete cooperation in the implementation of joint projects (for example, building a joint Israeli-Jordanian Red Sea–Dead Sea canal). This stage of development, though, can be fully implemented only when regional authoritative bodies are established. These organizations will plan and run the joint enterprises and ensure that all standards, specifications, and contracts are honored. Beyond the bilateral, and even the multilateral cooperation, on specific projects, the very existence of these regional bodies will bring stability to the region, attract foreign investment, and spur continued development.

Throughout history, the Middle East has been a key trade and communications link between East and West and North and South. The hostilities of modern times made borders impregnable, closing each side off from the other side of the world—both physically and ideologically—and preventing everyone from realizing the tremendous geographic advantages of the Middle East. Only with peace can these borders be transformed from barriers to bridges.

As we head toward this new era, whether at the early stage when border passage will be controlled and entry permits required, or at the final stage with open borders and freedom of movement, we need modern communications and transportation systems in the Middle East. We must follow the models of the United States and of Western Europe, which ended intracontinental estrangement and launched a new era of openness, in which ideas, people, and products could move freely from place to place. The possibility of nonstop transportation promotes activity and creativity. Peace will also attract travelers, either tourists who want to visit the region or those who want a convenient stopover. The infrastructure must be upgraded so that the Middle East can resume its historical position at the world's center.

GOOD planning requires that we define our ultimate goal and then structure our intermediate goals around it, based on the possibilities that can be realized at each stage. Here our objective is complete regional cooperation within a fixed, stable community, which will be responsible for a shared infrastructure. In transportation, this means constructing multinational seaports, airports, railways, and expressways that link the countries of the region and connect the region to Africa and Europe. A state-of-the-art regional transportation system will enable us to decrease the time and expense of travel or transport. Direct routes will shorten geographical distances and help create a sophisticated regional market. All roads lead to development. The more useful they are, the greater are the savings in lives, time, and money. Roads also help combat isolation.

RAILROADS

The Hejaz Railway, running from Medina in the south, by way of the Jordan valley, to Damascus in the north, with a connection to Haifa, operated until 1948, when it was partly dismantled at the outbreak of the Arab-Israeli wars. Some parts are still intact, a legacy of British imperialist rule in the region. The British laid the line from Egypt to Tripoli by way of Port Said, Haifa, and Beirut, and some local lines are still in use. According to Israeli estimates, this rail line can be refurbished in only six months.[1]

The line from Zemah to Haifa can be used to transport freight from the port of Haifa to Jordan and Syria. A parallel auxiliary line could be built along the Mediterranean coast. The project of rebuilding the sections destroyed by war, extending the track, and building additional lines and a second track present an industrial and economic challenge with the potential to generate substantial profits for both investors and users. A rapid modern railroad system would serve the very religious who make annual pilgrimages to the holy cities. It would, of course, also be used for family visits, vacations, and trips to the countryside. European tourists could travel from Turkey through Syria, Lebanon, Israel, Egypt, and other parts of Africa, or through Syria, Israel, Jordan, Saudi Arabia, and the Persian Gulf. The tracks will serve individual countries' ports on the Mediterranean and Red seas, multinational ports, and trade and holiday centers to be built in Gaza and along the planned Red Sea–Dead Sea canal.

ROADS

Along with development of the railroads, there are plans for three
expressway systems. One will cross the Middle East from North
Africa to Europe, along the sea (through Egypt, Israel, Lebanon,
Syria, and Turkey). The second will cross the Middle East from
North Africa to Iraq and the Persian Gulf. Both will enable private cars from Europe to reach Middle Eastern countries and
continue on to Africa, or vice versa. The third system will be a
series of connecting roads between Gaza and Hebron, Jerusalem
and Amman, Haifa and Mafraq (in Jordan), and Haifa and Damascus. These projects will be implemented partly by the participating countries and in part by international corporations that will
be granted the right to operate user-fee roads.

PORTS AND FREE TRADE AREAS

All countries of the region will be granted free access to the major
ports on the Mediterranean and along the Red Sea. Free trade
areas can be built adjacent to the ports of Latakia, Beirut, Haifa
(or Ashdod), Gaza, and Alexandria (or Port Said) on the Mediterranean, and Jidda on the Red Sea. A joint Eilat-Aqaba port
could also be established at the mouth of the Red Sea–Dead Sea
canal. The free trade area will house light industry, trade centers,
entertainment, and administrative and marketing services. In the
first stage, these areas will be under the jurisdiction of the countries in which they are located, but ultimately they will come under the centralized management of the regional community and
will receive interregional status. They, too, will contribute to sta-

bility in the Middle East and, like any other managerial organization, will be interested in maintaining the conditions that facilitate growth.

Two of the ports just mentioned are not yet in existence. At the moment, the port in Gaza is but a small, local fishing town, a reflection of the fate of the Gaza Strip throughout the period of Israeli–Palestinian hostilities. The area has great growth potential, and under peaceful conditions it can prosper, supplying jobs and income to thousands of families. It is no coincidence that the idea of a large port here has aroused the imagination of several foreign governments and European investors, and, as the process continues, we expect others to express interest. Modern technology can make the Gaza port one of the most useful on the Mediterranean coast. Merchandise and cargo will pass through its gates to points in Israel, Palestine, Jordan, Saudi Arabia, and even Iraq. It will bring an economic revolution to the entire region, especially to Palestinian residents. Once Gaza is a flourishing port, it can also be a terminus for road and rail systems, a regional fishing center, and a magnet for foreign investment.

Today, the crowded, neglected Gaza Strip has unacceptable health and sanitary conditions. It offers no source of income for the residents, who for decades have been hostages of the hostilities, captive from birth in a life of poverty, deprivation, and humiliation. With the coming peace and plans for the future, Gaza will again blossom, and its people will live in prosperity, honor, and plenty. As a coastal city, Gaza can also be an important tourist center, and a marina built around the new port will attract even more visitors.

Two ports sit on the northern coast of the Gulf of Eilat (Aqaba)—Eilat, which is Israeli, and Aqaba, which is Jordanian. Eilat and Aqaba are twin cities, stationed on either side of a sealed border. There is no exchange of gunfire between Israeli and Jordanian forces, and sometimes there are even signs of cooperation, but there is no direct contact or free passage between the two ports, the two cities, or the two countries. Only the mosquitoes fly freely back and forth to irritate residents, tourists, and port workers on both sides. This situation will change dramatically with the signing of the peace accord. When the walls of hostility and hatred come tumbling down, there will be no need for separate ports. Uniting them will enlarge the beach, improve the sea and land environments, and open the way for high-level cooperation between Israel and Jordan. The joint port will be established at the southern tip of the canal. Perhaps even in the first stage it can be jointly managed by representatives of both nations, under the supervision of an Eilat-Aqaba port authority. Later, the port and the free trade center (to be built at the port) will be operated by the regional system, with its independent port and air authorities. A common port here will also eliminate the need for an ecologically and economically costly railroad extension through the mountainous terrain that encircles these cities. Road and railroad junctions will be built adjacent to the free trade area, blending in with the unique international atmosphere in this area of perennial summer.

The Gulf of Eilat is at the juncture of Israel, Jordan, and Egypt, and it is not far from the Saudi Arabian border. This is an ideal location for a major international airport that will serve these four countries. The airport will transform the borders into bridges, uniting cultures, corporations, economic and trade systems, and, most important, people without regard to origin, religion, nationality, or gender.

CANAL

The Red Sea–Dead Sea canal is a large project that will take advantage of most of the blessings of peace. A joint port—a Port of Peace—will be built at the southern end.

The canal is a multipurpose project. It is intended to transport water from the Red Sea to the Dead Sea, replacing the water Israel and Jordan divert from the Jordan and Yarmuk rivers for irrigation. The water will also be used for research and development in pisciculture, to foster tourist services in the Israeli and Jordanian Arava, and to set up an infrastructure for further economic development in the Arava Depression. The water will cascade into the Dead Sea from the cliffs above, and the power generated by the difference in altitude will be harnessed for electricity. One possibility we should explore is desalination: a combined system of generating electricity and desalting some of the water used to manufacture electricity could lower the cost of desalination for other purposes.

Even those who do not accept Zionist teachings cannot but wonder at Theodore Herzl's vision of a Red Sea canal in his utopian work, *Old New Land.* Herzl pictured a dual-purpose canal that would transport water from the Mediterranean to the northern Dead Sea. Our design differs from his, and of course, our technological tools are far more sophisticated, but Herzl's original idea is surprisingly similar to the one we are considering more than ninety years later. On the very first page of his novel, he wrote, "If you will it, it is not a fairytale."[2]

Herzl describes a journey through the Land of Israel. The heroes reach Jericho, and some continue southward, to see the canal: "On the way from Jericho they had not had an unimpeded view of the sea, but now it all lay before them, as large as the lake of Geneva. They stood at the northern end, and to the right they saw a narrow tongue of land lying before the cliffs from which the waters of the Canal came rushing down. . . . Seeing the iron pipes which carried the canal water down on the turbines, Kingscourt was reminded of Niagara."[3] The guide explains the technology of bringing water from the Mediterranean and having it plunge into the Dead Sea, over 900 hundred feet below. This process generates electricity and replenishes the freshwater diverted from the Jordan for irrigation. The power stations attract industries, and the canal brings new life to the Dead Sea. About twenty large pipes conduct the water and turn the turbines. A rolling, thunderous din reverberates from the cascading water, and the air is filled with a white foamy spray.

At the end of the nineteenth century, it was fine to dream. At the end of the twentieth, it is time to transform the dream into reality.

The government of Israel has tried to fulfill Herzl's vision, but a canal along his chosen route was not economically feasible. This became clear only after a great deal of money had been invested. The Jordanians objected vociferously to the project, an exclusively Israeli experiment to change the topography of the Dead Sea unilaterally. Other proposals to dredge a canal from the Mediterranean Sea to the Jordan Valley were submitted, but no action was taken. Jordan wanted to build its own canal from the Red Sea, but Israel expressed disapproval. Eventually, both countries froze all plans to build a canal.

In the negotiations now being conducted between Israel and Jordan, the Red Sea–Dead Sea canal has been discussed as a joint project backed with international funding. Bolstering peace between Israel and Jordan, the canal would receive reasonable financing with international guarantees. The project requires a considerable investment—of at least $2 billion—for dredging the canal and building a hydroelectric plant, in addition to the cost of building a joint port, dismantling the ports currently operating, and cleaning up the Eilat-Aqaba shore. The entire project would take at least eight years, at which time the canal and port would be the Middle East's ticket to the twenty-first century.

The details are not yet fully formulated, but the main concept is clear: Israel and Jordan will lengthen the Eilat-Aqaba port and create an artificial bi-territorial gulf at the southern end of the two cities. On the gulf, Israel and Jordan will build their Port of Peace. Before the port goes into operation, the existing ports will be dismantled, as will the Eilat-Ashqelon oil line. Water for the canal will be drawn from the artificial port and propelled northward, along the length of the Arava Depression. With the help of several pumping stations, the water will reach heights of almost 720 feet. It will then travel east to Jordan and continue north to power three electrical generators. The water will then veer west, back toward Israel, where it will power another three electrical stations, wind around the potash pools of the Dead Sea industries, and enter the sea.

The canal will also benefit tourism (as detailed in the following chapter) and farmed fish production. Israeli experts foresee tremendous growth in fish farming, from almost no profits today to hundreds of millions of dollars annually within fifteen years.[4] This estimate is based on fishing conditions in the world and on the world fish market, particularly the European one, which is not meeting the rising demand for fish. To satisfy this demand, we must develop artificial lakes and ponds to breed fish. Since almost all the water needed for this new industry can be recycled (taken from the hydroelectric plant and later returned to it), fish farming will be a profitable by-product of the canal project and will require almost no additional capital. The water from the fish ponds will travel in the canal to the Dead Sea, where the organic matter in the water will decompose with help of naturally occurring bacteria and minerals. In contrast, development of fisheries on a similar scale in the Eilat-Aqaba gulf would contaminate the immediate environment and harm the flora and fauna of the Red Sea.

The ideas expressed here are not yet supported by detailed engineering and economic plans and are not ready for immediate implementation. A great deal of work awaits us, but we must take the first step while we have this chance to reach our goal. Politically, this earthshaking enterprise can help maintain peace and establish mutual long-term interests. This benefits not only the nations of the Middle East but those outside the region also. It was not an afterthought at the peace talks when the Italians started to investigate the economic feasibility of this canal project. But at the moment of truth, it will be necessary to consider all components and aspects of the canal. I believe it will be built. The water will flow along the Arava, the power stations will give light, and the wastelands will bloom with life. The region will experience peace, serenity, and progress. People from other countries will use the sea port and airport, visit the spas and vacation centers, and enjoy the products of our flourishing desert.

IN contrast to political history, nature has linked Israel and Jordan with four shared geographical assets: the Jordan River, the Dead Sea, the Arava Depression that lies between the Dead and Red Seas, and the Red Sea shore. Continued hostilities are liable to endanger all four assets and turn the Jordan River into a dry, historical memory, the Dead Sea into a bygone treasure, the Arava into an eternal desert, and the Red Sea into a God-given, squandered resource. Instead of fighting over the water flowing down the Jordan River, we can generate additional water and distribute it for the benefit of all. Cooperation will revitalize the Dead Sea and transform it into a tremendous source of income, benefiting Israel, Jordan, and the Palestinians. Alongside its curative powers and beauty aids, the sea produces potash, bromine, magnesium, and salt. The Arava—that long stretch of wilderness which already is dotted with flourishing settlements that grow out-of-season fruit—can attract tourists from all over the world. The dry, hot climate and unique scenery, which changes complexion with the coming of dawn and dusk, will be the backdrop for new lakes that will pepper the land as part of the canal project. Tourists will be astonished at the vivid, natural beauty of the area, which combines the near-forgotten aura of a primeval world with the conveniences of modern-day development. And the Red Sea is a shining jewel, resting in the shade of its crowning mountains, with magnificent coral and kaleidoscopic fish. No longer in anger and suspicion, but rather with hope and equanimity, the waves of the sea will lap against the sandy shore.

The Red Sea will change not only economically and ecologically but also strategically. Two wars have broken out because of attempts to close off the Strait of Hormuz. The Saudi Arabians directed most of their oil pipelines toward the Persian Gulf, until a bitter truth was revealed: until the Strait of Hormuz is no longer subject to the vagaries of Iranian and Iraqi rulers, the Persian Gulf will know no peace or security, equanimity or stability.

The situation is different in the Red Sea basin, where conditions are ripe for changing the Red Sea into a calm, blue body of water. The map shows that the western shores of the sea are lined with friendly countries: on the north, Israel is next to Egypt. Fif-

teen years after Camp David, we can declare the peace between
Israel and Egypt a success. Peace has not been officially declared
with Jordan, but there are strong glimmers among the sand dunes.
Israel has almost reached a general peace agreement with Jordan;
the king has hesitated to sign because he fears isolation from the
Arab world if first to do so. But peace is just a matter of time, and
relations are dictated by reason.

Reason is also the basis of our relationship with Saudi Arabia.
The kingdom lies adjacent to two countries that threaten its stability: Iraq on the north and Iran on the other side of the Persian
Gulf. Saudi Arabia has been doubly blessed—with great wealth
from tremendous oil reserves, and with central importance to the
millions of Muslims who visit the holy cities of Mecca and Medina
—and this continues to rankle jealous neighbors. Peace is vital to
Saudi Arabia, so it has no reason to be hostile toward Israel.

In the south, at the entrance to the Red Sea, is Yemen. This
country is currently undergoing fascinating changes. It recently
conducted free parliamentary elections and, in fact, fifty women
were elected—an event whose significance should not be underes-
timated. Even in the far depths of the country, echoes of a desire
for peace are reverberating, as proved by Yemen's recent agreement to allow Jews to emigrate. It is in Yemen's clear interest to
maintain security and fishing rights in the Red Sea. Yemen, too,
has no grievance with Israel.

And across the Red Sea from Yemen is the new nation of
Eritrea. Eritrea gained independence in 1993, and is led by a
young and intelligent leadership that wants to work for peace.

These countries can turn this important area around. The Red
Sea has central strategic value, so it can also be a gulf of true and
all-encompassing peace. We can already take cooperative actions
that will build trust, such as establishing reciprocal early warning

systems on military movements, with limitations on permissible military force and arms, or implementing joint projects to rescue fishermen and pilots. I am convinced that the Red Sea can be the springboard for a good arms control agreement. The sea can contribute to tourism (fishing and vacationing) as well as freight and oil transport. We can build long roads along its beaches, dig tunnels for transporting water, lay oil and gas pipelines, connect electrical and communications networks—and make the Red Sea a flourishing region for trade. The Red Sea is a long and narrow gulf. Because it is narrow, we can bridge it with peace.

11

THE DEVELOPMENT
OF TOURISM

TOURISM IS ONE OF THE MOST IMPORTANT
natural resources of the sun-soaked Middle East, an area that has
played a pivotal role in human history, culture, and religion.
Thanks to our ancestors' industriousness, resourcefulness, beliefs,
and art forms, the Middle East is a magnet for contemporary
tourists. They stand in awe before the permanence of Jerusalem,
the splendor and power of the Pyramids and the Sphinx, the
stunning perfection of Petra, the beauty and tranquillity of Baalbek, and the spiritual quality of the holy places.

The Middle East is a tourist's paradise, offering an entire spectrum of experience: the blazing sands of the desert and the lofty
snows of the Lebanese mountains; well-known rivers and water-

ways and eternal wilderness; picturesque villages straight out of
the pages of a history book and modern, noisy, crowded cities; the
solemnity of faith and the excitement of recreation. Tourists can
spend their days at the beaches—some beaches are hot and sunny,
even in the winter—and their nights at clubs, theaters, and con-
cert halls; in the winter, they can ski on Mount Hermon or enjoy a
day at a Dead Sea health spa. They can follow in the footsteps of
Moses, Jesus, Muhammad, or the prophets; they can visit the ancient sites and see with their own eyes where civilization began.

THE shared tradition of Jews, Christians, and Arabs tells of our
common ancestor, Abraham, who was renowned for his hospitality. Throughout history, Abraham's descendents have recognized
the importance of hospitality and have tried to emulate their ancestor. Today, against a backdrop of the technological revolution
that has radically changed transportation and communications
and has turned tourism into a popular commodity, waves of tourists should be coming to the Middle East, enjoying the historical
and religious sites and providing income for residents. Unfortunately, this is not the case. About 50 million tourists visit Spain
every year, while only 1.5 million go to Egypt. The number who
visit Syria is somewhat lower, while marginally more people visit
Israel. But it is obvious that the region has not fulfilled its potential for tourism.

The root of the problem is violence, with potential danger to
tourists caught in a conflict. Violence deters tourists, while the
threat of war is the very antithesis of conditions for tourism to
flourish. And not only do "big" wars hinder tourism; so do "little" wars and acts of terrorism. Thus terrorism, inspired by religious or political conflict, and terrorist actions directed against

tourists or tourist sites in particular, keep millions of people away from the Middle East every year. Fear inhibits Christian, Muslim, and Jewish pilgrims; holiday makers who want to spend their vacations in a peaceful location; people seeking their national, religious, or family roots; executives hoping to combine a business trip with relaxation; even individuals from overseas with family in the region, who want to celebrate holidays with their relations.

Until the 1970s, tourism was a major source of income for Lebanon. Since then, however, tourism to that country has been completely destroyed, owing to civil war and Lebanon's transformation into a base of operations for terrorist organizations. The Lebanese tragedy in the Land of the Cedars is the most striking example of how terror and tension obstruct tourism. More recently, fundamentalist extremists targeting tourists in Egypt have aggravated the economic crisis of the largest and oldest Arab nation—a nation with elements of both East and West and whose tourist sites could attract tens of millions of tourists every year.[1]

Thus, were it not for the violence, tourism could become an immediate source of income, supporting millions of families in the region. Peace and tourism go hand-in-hand—in ending the difficulties we face now and in supplying the tremendous opportunity for the future. To develop the tourist industry, to attract investment and encourage tourists to travel throughout the world, we must have tranquillity, calm, a genuine peace; conversely, the development of tourism and the arrival of tourists, apart from financial ramifications, can act as a stabilizing force, creating genuine interest in preserving peace in the region.

Several factors will help tourists to the Middle East: open borders, a sophisticated transportation and communications infrastructure, joint marketing of popular tour packages, and a well-developed tourist industry, including new tourist attractions.

Open Borders

After peace is established, national borders will be opened, even if passport control remains necessary in the beginning, as established by the peace agreement between Israel and Egypt. Opening the borders alone will help revive tourism among Middle Eastern nations. However, the principal gain will be an upsurge in foreign tourists, who will be able to visit different states in the region, taking in several attractions in one trip. Most of these tourists will come from North America, Europe, and the Far East. Boosting tourism from North America and the Far East depends largely on choosing and implementing the correct marketing campaign. Successful European tourism also depends on developing an overland transportation infrastructure.

Infrastructure

Even before the establishment of a formal regional framework, we can begin to draw up plans for upgrading our infrastructure and developing interstate overland transportation routes, especially between Europe and the Middle East. When it is possible to travel from Europe to the Middle East by train or car, many tourists will spend long weekends in the region, in addition to those making longer visits. A travel infrastructure depends, of course, on opening borders, and creating a vested interest in keeping the borders open.

Tour Packages

A new international company could be established to market Middle Eastern tour packages in North America, Europe, and the Far East, offering trips to multiple Middle Eastern destinations (for example, Egypt, Israel, Jordan, Lebanon, and Syria). Our focus is on budget travelers, who constitute the most promising market segment. But we have to guarantee those travelers maximum return on their investment. Packages with multiple destinations do just this, and also encourage tourists' friends and acquaintances to visit the area. We need not wait until the regional framework is in place. As early as the negotiation stage, we can direct our energy, resources, and creative thinking toward this promising goal in anticipation of the establishment of peace. Then these plans can be put into effect the moment the peace agreements are signed.

Tourist Attractions

Some local development projects will automatically attract tourists, such as the fishing port at Gaza, the Port of Peace at Eilat-Aqaba, and the Red Sea–Dead Sea canal. Other areas can also be developed specifically for this purpose, from vacation villages to luxury hotels and recreation facilities. The joint company set up to market tour packages will be able to attract foreign investment in developing the tourism infrastructure. Particularly, Middle East tourism has a tremendous economic potential as well as other important qualities, making it a prime target for foreign investors. Some countries in the region will need to build hotels and vacation villages for the budget traveler; others must provide paved access roads to existing tourist attractions or develop existing ski slopes, sailing centers, and other recreational facilities. These can also be developed by multinational companies, with requisite funding. Once again, we must have peace and calm to attract this investment; in turn, this investment will be a stabilizing influence in the region. A man to a man is a wolf, wrote Hobbes. The future Middle East should become a place where a person to a person is a host, not a hostage.

12

The World of
Tomorrow

IN THE DAYS OF STALIN, SOVIET PROPA-
ganda described the Soviet Union as "the world of tomorrow"—
an attempt to present the Kremlin-led transition to socialism as an
unavoidable historical necessity. But history has taken a completely different course. The faulty execution of the communist
dream, and the misguided attempts to impose communism
through brute force and cruel repression, illustrate the fallacy of a
supposed historical necessity. The world of tomorrow—the world
of our children and grandchildren—will bear no resemblance to
the world Lenin envisioned and Stalin tried to create. The principles of totalitarian power will not stand at the center of tomor-

row's world. Rather, the principles of meritocracy—leadership based on knowledge attained at universities and research institutes—will predominate. The national or class collective will not constitute the basis of social organization. Rather, the individual will assume responsibility. National goals will no longer be based on control or territorial expansion, but on improving the quality of life, raising the standard of living, and increasing life expectancy. Twenty-first-century people will reach the goals of social welfare and social justice out of a concern for individual justice. As a consequence, economics will carry more weight than politics in international relations.

Until the end of the twentieth century, the general concept of history was rooted in the European model of national politics, springing from the world of nationalist values and symbols. The next era will be increasingly based on the Asiatic model of national politics, drawn from the world of economic values, whose fundamental principle is exploitation of knowledge in order to maximize profit. This is how Japan became an economic superpower after World War II. And this is how smaller and somewhat less ambitious countries—South Korea, Singapore, Taiwan, and Hong Kong—have made the transition from developing nations to economic powers with trade surpluses. Even the tariffs some Western nations imposed to compete with these new "Asian tigers" have not slowed the growth of these countries. China and India—two giant nations with large internal "common markets" —are now starting out on this promising road. Soon Vietnam, still recovering from its war wounds, and Thailand and North Korea will join the Asian club.

The economic success experienced by these Asian states stems from two key strategic decisions: to automate factories and computerize service industries, and to entitle all citizens to education and computer training. The computer revolution is even more far-reaching than was the printing revolution, which ushered in the Enlightenment and held out the possibility of universal literacy. Since Johannes Gutenberg, the inventor of movable type, one person has been able to communicate with many others. Now the process is accelerating. We have the means to expand horizons and create whole new worlds of information, communications, and creativity.

In 1987, shortly after the end of my term as Prime Minister of the national unity government, I visited the Robotics Institute at Carnegie-Mellon University in Pittsburgh. There I met with scholars and researchers who are integrating computers with philosophy in an attempt to break through the existing boundaries of understanding and knowledge. Among them was Professor Herbert Simon, recipient of the 1978 Nobel Prize for Economics— one of the founders of political science and the man who has done more than anyone else to develop the new and promising field of artificial intelligence. The French author Jean-Jacques Servan-Schreiber was also present, as head of the Center for Computer Study in Paris, and he recorded my conversation with Simon:

SIMON: In understanding the human brain, we have to find ways to make our thinking more efficient—in education, in the ability to create intellectually. We brought these ideas to Peking, where we are preparing a three-year course based on learning by example, without a teacher. The result: the students who participated in this course did better than others, and actually finished the work in two years instead of the planned three years.

PERES: How can we take advantage of this new idea?

SIMON: We can design a computer course that carries out teaching functions: to use the computer in order to understand ourselves. In this way, we can improve our thinking. In the next stage perhaps the computers will be able to think. This introduces a philosophical question: is there any justification for seeing human beings as chosen individuals? We have to explore our place in the broader system of existence. The problem is not how to separate ourselves from nature, but how to unite with nature. We have to see ourselves in the framework of a broader, greater world, and learn how to live with it in peace.

PERES: You're saying that this technology has potential applications in two fields: teaching and decision making.

SIMON: Yes. In fact, specialized systems are already being used to make decisions on a large scale. A type of "employed" computer program is used widely in industry, and it makes decisions at an expert level.

PERES: Can the computer predict the results of its decisions? Can it do better than the human brain?

SIMON: It can only predict if there is a good, valid theory in the relevant field. When an engineer designs a motor he can accurately state how the motor will function. But if somebody tells you to act in accordance with a particular economic strategy, neither the computer nor the economist can promise that the predictions will be on target. As you know, there simply isn't a satisfactory theory for this.

PERES: This is because the economy is highly dependent on psychology. No computer can provide the cumulative

psychological reaction of the public, because economic behavior greatly depends on expectations.

SIMON: The recent developments in mathematics have
made us rather pessimistic about our ability to predict,
even at the level of pure logic. Today there is a mathematical theory, called "chaos theory," that proves that even
mathematical systems can behave in unpredictable ways.

PERES: That's extremely interesting. I now realize that we
can't blame ourselves for becoming more and more skepti-
cal and doubtful.

SIMON: Maybe, in some fields.[1]

Professor Simon has achieved an unprecedented breakthrough: its
likely that when we finally understand how artificial intelligence
works, we will also understand how the human brain functions.
This will unlock the secret of existence of the new world—the
world of tomorrow.

The next day I discussed my conversation with Simon with
Servan-Schreiber. I told him that Carnegie-Mellon was unique,
because of its multidimensional challenge, from philosophy to industry, through education. We have neither the time nor the pa-
tience to learn slowly and prepare for the new era that is arriving
rapidly. We must immediately start to train personnel for every
field, in anticipation of the next stage; any delay will threaten the
future. The computer revolution also means that all individuals
will have the opportunity to make their own decisions, since they
possess the tool that can supply the necessary information. Wisdom is, at the very least, a collection of information. The knowledge is available, the equipment and machines are constantly

getting smaller, and the required financial outlay is diminishing. Perhaps this will mean the end of the era of mass production—the legacy of the industrial revolution—and the start of small-scale production. In agriculture, the size of the field determines neither the yield nor the quality of produce. It is the knowledge invested that determines the results.

From this we can conclude that a nation's prosperity no longer depends so heavily on its natural resources and extensive territory, or on its concentration of wealth. A nation's prosperity is a product of the accumulation of knowledge. This is true wealth at the turn of the twenty-first century, the threshold of tomorrow's world. And it all hinges on the development of scientific ideas that have technological applications. An amazingly small amount of money is needed to create innovative and sophisticated new technologies and products.

THE Middle East can apply the lessons of both the computer revolution and the rise of Asian economic power. To do this, its leaders must abandon the conflicts of yesterday and invest in education instead of the arms race. The knowledge revolution must begin in the schools. Today, education starts with an individual's first breath and continues lifelong. To progress, we must allow no gaps in our education—the education we receive and the education we give our children and grandchildren must be ongoing. Education is a continuous, prolonged, dynamic process. The Russian writer Maksim Gorky said, "My life is my university." Today we should say, "My university is my life."

Education has two fundamental aspects: the accumulation and transmission of knowledge, and the development of traditions and values. The first element is universal: there is no difference between the "Arab" knowledge of Avicenna, the "Polish" knowledge of Copernicus, or the "Jewish" knowledge of Einstein. In contrast, differences in traditional values have national, religious, historical, and ethnic significance. The ethic we inherited from the Enlightenment is an openness and readiness to recognize different values and to find the common denominator that unites all people. But a specific national or religious ethic is difficult to share with all people and all religions. Perhaps its time has not yet come. Nevertheless, once peace has been established in our region, there is a place for scientific, technological, and educational cooperation in transmitting practical knowledge—the knowledge that will help us all to produce our daily bread. Eventually, we will recognize the common characteristics that unite all people and thus see beyond our national or religious barriers. But to achieve this intellectual openness we must have genuine peace, to overcome the emotional obstacles that have resulted from a century of conflict. Indeed, educational cooperation, coupled with recognition of our neighbors and acceptance of the legitimacy of our different experiences and presence, will ensure that the next generation knows how to maintain peace. Then peace can open the gates to the newly discovered fields of reason, values, and knowledge.

13

CONFEDERATION

THE DICTATES OF LOCAL GEOGRAPHY, AS well as the wars and their aftermath, have made the Palestinian problem seem almost insoluble. I have rejected this view because it substitutes apathy for creativity and places obstacles in the way of progress. The more elusive the solution, the greater the challenge. Instead of giving way to despair, we must harness our intelligence and creativity to surmount both imaginary obstacles and real impediments.

UNTIL the 1948 War of Independence, the Palestinian people did not exist as a separate entity, either in their own consciousness or in the minds of other people, including the Arab nations. During the Ottoman Empire, national identity was a minor consideration in the mind-set of its peoples, as well as of those in the broader domestic and international scene. When nationalism began to take root in the Middle East—at the time the peace treaties were signed at the end of World War I[1]—the region experienced two parallel trends: a unifying, pan-Arab movement, which regarded Arab ethnicity as a nationalist identity; and a leaning toward particularism, which emphasized the unique history and culture of each Arab state. The Palestinians viewed themselves as Arabs. During the British Mandate, Palestinian nationalist consciousness was defined as being part of the greater Arab nation, giving Palestinians a different, separate identity from that of the Jews living in the region. It was no coincidence that they chose the slogan PALESTINE IS ARAB. Rather than claim ownership of the land in the name of a particularist nationality, they did so in the name of pan-Arabism. They also asked for and received Arab solidarity before the 1948 war, on ideological grounds of unification, not a particular national identity.

An attempt to combine these general and particularist nationalist trends is found in the PLO's Palestinian Covenant, which asserts that Palestine is the national homeland of the Palestinian Arab people; it is an integral part of the Arab homeland, and the Palestinian people are an integral part of the Arab nation. In other words, even the founding document of the Palestinian national movement does not lay claim to the land on behalf of Palestinians alone. The term *Palestine* in English, or *Falastin* in Arabic, signifies a place and not a people. A Palestinian state never actually existed; and only during the ideological struggle against the State of Israel and the Zionist movement did the ideologues of the Palestinian camp begin to speak about a specific historical Palestinian connection to this controversial land, a connection that is independent of any pan-Arab context. At that time, the Palestinians began to be described as the descendents of the ancient Jebusites, and some even suggested that the Palestinian people have existed "from time immemorial."[2]

These facts do not question the legitimacy of Palestinian national consciousness. The modern democratic outlook recognizes the validity of forming a new national association, termed "people building" in the professional literature, based on the consciousness of independence by any group that establishes such a national association. The Palestinians became a people when they decided to do so and when they began to act as a national collective.[3] Questions of how they began to act as a national collective and what factors led to this awakening are of interest to historians and sociologists, but the speculations make no difference in determining strategy. Strategy depends on present reality, not on scenarios that might have been possible under different conditions. Even if we agree that the rise of Palestinian nationalism was a reaction to Zionist activity, the fact remains that a Palestinian national identity now exists and plays a central role in the political arena, both regionally and worldwide. Just as we Jewish people did not ask the Palestinians for permission to become a state, neither do they need our permission to become a people. However, the relationship between this national identity and the territorial unit called *Eretz Yisrael,* or the Land of Israel, is complex, and a complex problem requires a complex solution.

THE British captured the country called Palestine from the Turks in 1917. Five years later, it was divided: the Hashemite kingdom was established east of the Jordan River, and Palestine was established west of the Jordan, under a mandate granted to Great Britain by the League of Nations. Other partitions and suggestions for partition were proposed after this division. The partition proposed by the United Nations in 1947 was designed to establish two states, one Arab and the other Jewish. Most of the mountainous areas and the eastern part of Palestine was intended to be the Arab state. (The United Nations decision spoke of an "Arab state," not of a "Palestinian state.") Only a small part of the territory along the coast, in the valleys, and in the Negev was designated as the Jewish state.

The leaders of the Jewish population in the country were not overjoyed at the partition decision, but they agreed to it. David Ben-Gurion understood that political independence for the Jewish people inevitably meant partition between Jews and Arabs, on the basis of an inevitable and realistic compromise. He concluded that neither side could realize all its national aspirations, and that some goals must be sacrificed to realize other goals. If Ben-Gurion had had a realistic-minded Arab counterpart, it is likely that the history of the Middle East would have been very different.

But history is not made of *ifs*. The Arab leaders made an error of judgment: they rejected the United Nations map and went to war. At the end of the war a new reality had been created, reflected in a new map: Israel gained territory while Jordan, which had fought in the war, controlled the area of the projected Arab state. After the cease-fire agreement with Israel, King Abdullah ibn Hussein decided to annex the territories he had conquered, convened the Council of Notables, and obtained their consent. Since then, the territory of the planned Arab state has become known as the West Bank (of the Jordan River). The Palestinian residents of the West Bank received Jordanian citizenship and some gradually began to serve as important officials in the political and economic life of the Jordanian kingdom.

Change of even greater significance occurred in the wake of the 1967 Six-Day War. Israel did not want to fight Jordan, and on the day the war broke out, Prime Minister Levi Eshkol sent two messages to King Hussein—one via the United States and the other via the United Nations—in which he explicitly promised that if Jordan did not initiate any hostile action, Israel would not attack. The messages were not understood in the sense that Israel had intended them, however. Jordan entered the war and lost the battle. (Not long ago, King Hussein said that his participation in the 1967 war was one of the two greatest mistakes he had made in his forty-year rule.) Israel won the war and captured the West Bank.

These two wars led to migrations. Arab refugees left their homes and fled the fighting as early as 1948. The refugees who stayed in the West Bank or crossed the Jordan River became Jordanian citizens, but most of them continued to live in the refugee camps that the United Nations Works and Relief Agency had set up. Many refugees did not get into these camps, and fled to Gaza, Lebanon, and other destinations.

More refugee migration followed the 1967 war. Some residents of the West Bank again crossed the river and sought refuge in Jordan. A few returned to their towns and villages after the fighting stopped, while others remained refugees. After the Six-Day War, Jewish settlements were begun in the vicinity of Jerusalem, in Judea and Samaria, and even in the Gaza Strip, altering the demographic profile of the outskirts of Jerusalem, the Jordan Valley, and the western foothills of Samaria. The refugees remain in a temporary situation that must be changed, for both political and humanitarian reasons. The solution has not yet been found, and the fate of these refugees has been tossed back and forth between nations. In large part, Arab countries have chosen to maintain the status quo in order to use these refugees as political ammunition against Israel.

The wars led to new demographics for the region and new

citizenship for the residents. They brought a new national texture to small, densely populated areas. The tragic aspect is that in politics, as in the kitchen, it is easy to break eggs and make omelets, but impossible to turn the omelets back into whole eggs. The wars only complicated an otherwise hostile situation. Furthermore, the conflicts left certain ideas and impressions in everyone's national consciousness—bad impressions that now will be very difficult to change. Continued wars and hostile actions, the many dead and wounded, and readiness to counterattack have made national security the determining factor. For almost half a century, Israel's leaders have been guided by the fear that an aggressive coalition of countries might launch a sudden war of annihilation. The Palestinians are concerned that they might once again become refugees, fleeing for their lives and wandering from place to place. Is it any wonder that the dream of "liberating the conquered lands" has become their central national goal?

War has solved nothing. Should we use force to settle the conflicts and disputes that force has so far been unable to resolve? Or should we look for a solution based on understanding—a creative solution to the minor conflicts that make up the major conflict, much like the Russian *matryoshka,* the wooden doll that contains an identical but smaller doll, which contains another smaller doll, which contains yet another smaller doll.

T H E contradiction between Israel's yearning for security and the Palestinian people's hope of "liberating the conquered lands" cannot be resolved by simple geography. Israel needs strategic depth, and the Palestinians claim exactly the same territory that is necessary to ensure Israel's strategic depth. In Israeli eyes, the map of their country looks like an anorexic body: tall and narrow-hipped. Narrow hips can be broken by a sudden, well-organized attack. So Israel's opposition to the establishment of a Palestinian state is a direct result of this fear. Even if the Palestinians agree that their state would have no army or weapons, who can guarantee that a Palestinian army would not be mustered later to encamp at the gates of Jerusalem and the approaches to the lowlands? And if the Palestinian state would be unarmed, how would it block terrorist acts perpetrated by extremists, fundamentalists, or irredentists?

The Palestinians claim that Israel's refusal to carry out all the provisions of UN Security Council Resolution 242 is proof that Israel does not intend to return significant areas to the Palestinian people. When the sentence about "territories in exchange for peace" was erased from the declaration of principles, the Palestinians interpreted this change as indisputable proof of their deepest fears.

The proposed interim solution—autonomy, beginning with the Gaza Strip and Jericho—is intended to change that political-psychological climate, thick with memories and threats. At first glance, the idea has merit. However, difficulties emerged early in the negotiations, as we traveled from the freezing climate of suspicion and fear to the warmth of understanding and reconciliation. The main problem was the definition of the autonomous territory. Both sides expressed reluctance to see a definition set the precedent for the territorial section of the permanent agreement. The fact that the permanent solution is still amorphous only increases mutual suspicion and fears.

Nevertheless, I believe that without progress in solving the Palestinian problem, we will not resolve the Arab-Israeli conflict. And if this conflict is not resolved, it will be very difficult—if not impossible—to build a new Middle East. Is it not time to find a permanent solution to the Palestinian problem? The answer is yes, and we have just begun to do so.

W E have to begin to grapple with the principal components of the Palestinian problem: borders, organization, and government.

The Borders

Future borders have always been and remain the thorniest aspect of the solution. One nation cannot rule over another against its will. The borders must, therefore, reflect population distributions as they exist today. Unfortunately, the picture is complicated. Apart from mutual suspicions, we must remember that the Israelis and Palestinians both consider the land between the Jordan River and the sea to be their historical homeland. Both nations consider their national and personal identity bound up with the historical significance of their land. Many Jews and Palestinians are not prepared to compromise as regards their historical rights; they believe they have an exclusive national right that contradicts and invalidates the claims of others. Thus every attempt to demarcate borders will inevitably touch a nerve, whether for strategic, national, or religious reasons. The sensitivity of both sides is so great that even a simple formula could become the recipe for renewed conflict.

Strategically, Israel is concerned with its advance line of defense. The defense line has to start at the Jordan River, to allay fears of possible aggression directed at the narrow "hips" of the state. The Palestinians focus on nationalism and point to the demographics of the West Bank and Gaza, which, even after the Likud government's intensive settlement policy, are 90 percent

Palestinian. It is obvious that Jerusalem, the Holy City, is sacred to all religions. It is the very heart of the Jewish people, the object of the prayers, dreams, and hopes of redemption after two thousand years of exile. Jerusalem is also holy to Christians and Muslims. Events central to the three monotheistic religions occurred in Jerusalem, influencing the development of each faith and forging close ties between the faithful and the holy places. And this is true not only of Jerusalem but of many other places in Israel, a country with many sites sacred to pilgrims.

This discussion is not limited to emotions, symbols, and historical heritage. I do not believe in the meaningless slogan JORDAN IS PALESTINE, which avoids recognizing the Palestinian problem as a national problem and dismisses any peaceful solution. However, from a strictly nationalist viewpoint, the fact that most inhabitants of Jordan are of Palestinian origin cannot be ignored, and this could cause unrest in the kingdom and disturb the stability of the entire region.

If this were not enough, we must also consider one of the most intractable objective difficulties in our warm region: the problem of water. Water moves underground, without revealing its presence to past or future mapmakers. The inevitable conclusion is that a simple territorial partition is a simple and untenable approach. Border lines cannot be drawn without first agreeing on the nature of the border.

We need soft borders, not rigid, impermeable ones. Borders are not walls. We need not close ourselves off with a wall, which in any case would not strengthen the national sovereignty of either side. Moses, Jesus, and Muhammad could not have read the writings of Hugo Grotius, the seventeenth-century thinker who introduced the concept of "sovereignty" to jurisprudence, diplomatic history, and the political lexicon. At the threshold of the twenty-first century, we do not need to reinforce sovereignty, but rather to strengthen the position of humankind—to permit direct contact and to adapt local reality to goals for the future.

By definition, a "soft" border is open to movement. Both secular and religious considerations force the residents of the Holy Land—Jordanians, Palestinians, and Israelis—to allow the free movement of people, ideas, and goods. From the economic standpoint, this is the best way to develop tourism on a large scale; this is the only way to equitably solve the problem of distributing water; and this is the most efficient way to develop agriculture and industry that can compete successfully in world markets.

The soft border is also valuable from a religious standpoint, since this is the only way to grant all people access to every holy place and house of prayer, so they may pray and experience spiritual exaltation. While insisting on preserving Jerusalem's status as a united city under Israeli control, Israel fully understands the Holy City's significance to Christians and Muslims as well as to Jews. The general consensus in Israel is that Jerusalem should be under Israeli political control, but the city will be open to all believers, of all faiths and nationalities. Perhaps this is the modern context for Zechariah's ancient prophecy "Jerusalem shall be inhabited without walls" (Zechariah 2:4). The wall Sultan Süleiman constructed on the foundations of King Herod's wall will continue to adorn Old Jerusalem, but it will not bar anyone from reaching any place in the Holy City. And the joyful prayer of the Jewish cantor, the Muslim muezzin, and the Christian choir will always rise from Jerusalem. This will be true for the other holy places throughout the country, too. Nowhere in the world is there a country quite like the land of Israel, where so many weapons and so many holy places occupy such a small area.

Now we must strive for fewer weapons and more faith. Soft,

open political boundaries will make it easier to reach an agreement and will help it withstand stormy times. These soft borders will also be valuable strategically. The Camp David agreement and the peace treaty between Israel and Egypt would never have been realized if the two states had not agreed to demilitarize the Sinai Peninsula. This was to the strategic advantage of both sides: Israel could not agree to have the Egyptian army hold the Sinai Desert, as it did on the eve of the Six-Day War; and Egypt could not permit the Israeli army to remain there, as was the case after the war. This created an objective situation, which calmed the fears of both sides. The demilitarization of Sinai eliminated one of the main factors that had led to the Six-Day War and one of its most tangible results.

The impressive achievements of the peace agreements between Israel and Egypt are extremely instructive: demilitarization best meets the needs and wishes of both sides. This lesson can help politicians establish the future of Judea, Samaria, and the Gaza Strip. The demilitarization of these areas (except for the Israeli security areas, as agreed at Camp David, though not yet appearing on the map) will be the optimal strategic solution to guarantee each side their minimum needs.

The Structure

The nature of soft borders necessitates that we agree not only on basic security but also on the political structure to be established in the areas under discussion. The political structure best suited to the limitations and possibilities of the area is a Jordanian-Palestinian confederation for political matters, and a Jordanian-Palestinian-Israeli "Benelux" arrangement for economic affairs, where an economic triangle will be the roof and the bilateral

framework the floor. I have been supporting a Jordan-Palestine
confederation for over twenty years.[4] In its most mature form, it
would be the optimum solution for the three sides involved—the
Jordanians, the Palestinians, and the Israelis—allowing each to
live in peace and prosperity without sacrificing their beliefs and
opinions. An agreement on political negotiation could be based
on this idea.

A confederation is the structure that will best allow the
Hashemite kingdom and the Palestinian entity to live together in
peace, without one side undermining the other. In the wake of
wars, sabotage, and terrorist acts, it does not take much imagination to see the value of this arrangement. Why do we have to wait
for violence? Is bloodshed the prerequisite for a political solution? Prevention is better than a cure.

The Jordanians and Palestinians have no option but to coexist.
The new political structure must faithfully reflect the demographic picture, which currently forces both sides to live under a
single political roof. Many Palestinians live in Jordan and even
serve as Jordanian officials with the permission of the government.
Most of the Palestinians who live in the territories hold Jordanian
passports; some of them even receive salaries from the royal trea-
sury. The differences between the Jordanian and Palestinian peoples do not stem from cultural, religious, traditional, or ethnic
differences. They are divided by arbitrary historical circumstances
and political events. Beyond the particularist national identities of
the Jordanians and the Palestinians, which reflect what divides
and distinguishes them, they have a common origin, which reflects
the aspect that unites them.

The soft border means that armies do not have to be stationed
right next to the border, as is customary in states divided by hard
borders. Thus, in a Jordanian-Palestinian confederation, the confederate army would be stationed east of the Jordan River. The

West Bank would be demilitarized, allowing Israel to make a logical response to territorial claims, since this arrangement would
also ensure Israel's strategic depth. The demilitarization arrangement and its joint supervision would be negotiated between the
sides, in order to increase mutual trust and prevent situations that
could endanger the stability of the peace.

An announcement of readiness to establish a Jordanian-
Palestinian confederation would generate new support, in spite of
earlier opposition. Many people in Jordan, in the Palestinian
camp, and in Israel would support this notion, if for no other
reason than to prevent the establishment of a separate, permanent
Palestinian state in Judea, Samaria, and Gaza. A separate Palestinian state would be received with unease, either overtly or covertly,
among Jordanians, and would face fierce opposition from Israelis.
Further, there would be widespread doubt as to whether a separate Palestinian state in such a small and problematic area could
actually survive and develop. In contrast, confederation might be
more acceptable to the Israelis (as it would not involve a separate
Palestinian state), more reasonable to the Jordanians (for the same
reason), and more promising for the Palestinians (as it would entail explicit consideration of the territorial aspect of the permanent solution).

There is a semantic, or quasi-semantic, argument concerning
the word *confederation*. In Israel, some claim that the concept
signifies a covenant between two independent states, so that a
Jordanian-Palestinian confederation would mean the establishment of a Palestinian state, separate from and independent of the
Hashemite kingdom. This interpretation does not, however, reflect the real nature of a confederation. To fully understand the
idea of confederation, it must be compared to the concept of a
federation.

Federalism is a concept that bases political organization on the geographic decentralization of political authority and its activities. The federal state is made up of autonomous regional states having representative institutions, thus constituting the inner link between a federal state and a democracy. A federal state may be distinguished from a standard state by three characteristics: the granting of a high degree of autonomy to the regions, the equal status of the regions and their powers in a permanent constitution, and the formation of the central government in such a way that includes the participation and influence of the various regions.

The difference between a federation and a confederation is linked to the legal status of local law: in a federation, federal law takes precedence over local law, since sovereignty rests with the federal structure. In short, the constituent regions receive only what the central authority gives them. In a confederation, the situation is reversed: the provisions of federal law are made valid through the agreement of the constituent regions, which themselves are sovereign, and federal law is valid as long as it does not contradict local law. The independence of regional units is greater than it would be in a federation, although just as in a federation, national security and foreign relations are entrusted exclusively to the central government. The Helvetian confederation—Switzerland—has lasted for five hundred years, a covenant with cantons rather than states. The cantons have considerable autonomy, but the Swiss state is represented worldwide by diplomats who are answerable to the confederate government, as is the minister for the disciplined and efficient Swiss army.

Some Palestinians agree with Yasser Arafat that a confederate arrangement is a satisfactory solution, but this would only be possible after declaration of a Palestinian state, even, as the saying goes, "if only for five minutes." If we agree on the best structure, we can get the stopped clock ticking again.

Government

No less important is the nature of the government to be established in the confederation. There is a built-in link between a confederation and democracy, since in an undemocratic regime authority is concentrated and not decentralized, and there are considerable restrictions on local government and representation. Jordan is a constitutional monarchy whose royal family has decided to allow people to hold democratic elections and to organize political parties, even if their platforms do not match the king's ideas. Jordan thus seems ripe for federalist development.

The Palestinian situation is more complicated. They have a coalition headed by the PLO, which was not elected. This PLO-led coalition must contend incessantly with a dozen rejectionist organizations, some of which are linked to headquarters in Damascus while others take orders from the spiritual leadership in Teheran. Since neither Arafat's coalition nor the opposition was elected, the Palestinians tend to resort to bullets rather than to ballots. The constant threat is that the gun, rather than the majority, will decide their fate.

The PLO is hampered three ways in its struggle with the opposition group Hamas: propaganda, funding, and terror. Hamas can employ superficial, demagogic language since, unlike the PLO, its representatives bear no responsibility for negotiations. This lack of responsibility makes things easier for the Hamas propaganda system, and makes the PLO's situation even worse.

And Hamas's financial situation is also better. It has a greater income than other organizations, with fewer financial obligations. It receives its funds from religious sources and distributes them only to its supporters. The PLO is now the victim of a boycott by oil-producing states (following Arafat's support of Saddam Hussein in the 1991 Persian Gulf War), while it must support the families of *intifada* victims and the Palestinian institutions that it has established, so that it can make its voice heard and prepare for the future.

Clearly, shots echo much more loudly than words. Hamas conducts its "public relations" through terror, and does not balk at using any means. Some people are impressed by this sort of terrorism, regarding it as a tool for realizing Allah's word on earth. The Palestinians, however, have begun to understand that they cannot simultaneously employ strategies of terror and negotiation; they must either talk or shoot. In any case, they see that it is very difficult to persuade Israel by shooting—even more difficult than competing with Hamas.

The best means the Palestinian organizations have available to overcome Hamas is via elections: they must create the authority of an elected majority against an armed and fanatical minority. If the Palestinians hold elections and the PLO ceases being a terrorist organization to become a political party, it will no longer be possible to ignore a democratically elected political organization. The elections in Jordan and among the Palestinians should also create a democratic basis for the Jordanian-Palestinian confederation. This development would lead to a division of power based on ideology and present needs, rather than on historical issues and obsolete realities.

Nothing can better serve the Arab world, and particularly the Palestinian people, than genuine democratization. The greatest error of the Arab people in the twentieth century—an error that has not yet been rectified—has been their affinity for totalitarian militaristic or presidential regimes. These regimes may talk persuasively about the people and the general good, but they do very little for them. They offer no hope of economic or social development, and they have done little to develop the Arab world. The individual Arab and Muslim believer has, more than anything else, been the victim of regressive oppression.

The lack of democracy has also helped foster the rise of fundamentalism, which threatens the stability of existing regimes in the Arab world. Ultimately, if the leaders of the Arab states do not adopt democracy, they will lose power. Either fundamentalist fanatics will take over their countries, or Arab youth will search for their own entrance ticket to the modern world—a democratic, free, prosperous world that is changing and progressing, which, like a great river, sweeps away all obstacles in its path.

FROM a political viewpoint, nothing can ensure peace and stability in the Middle East more than neighborly relations between states that differ in their national identities and heritages, but are united by the rule of democracy. Democracy is not just a method to ensure equality for every problem, but also a method to ensure equal rights to be different.

The twentieth century has proved the moral ascendancy of democracy and its social power. All the regimes of totalitarian oppression that have threatened democracy have themselves collapsed and fallen. The democratic way is the best method of bringing economic prosperity, stable peace, and freedom to every individual and every people. Democracy is like fresh air—available to every human being. Both are free of charge, but not necessarily used properly.

14

THE REFUGEE
PROBLEM

NO REASONABLE HUMAN BEING CAN REMAIN
indifferent to the plight of refugees. Whatever the reason for their
situation, the picture is the same: men, women, and children fleeing in fear of their lives, with terror in their eyes and despair in
their faces. They are abandoning their possessions, their past, the
place to which they are tied and from which they are being torn.
Some refugees are escaping from a sudden natural disaster—vol-
canic eruptions, earthquakes, floods. Some are fleeing more gradual natural catastrophes, such as drought, which force people and
animals from their homes and compel them to wander over barren
wastelands in search of water and food. And some seek refuge
from the deadly and destructive horrors of war.

Humankind has not yet found an adequate defense against sudden natural disasters. The penniless refugees fleeing earthquakes or floods are the victims of nature; no one can prevent these disasters or assign society responsibility for the tragedy, though society does have a duty to help the victims rehabilitate themselves. The situation is different for gradually occurring natural disasters, especially prolonged drought. Agricultural technology, desalination, and hydraulic engineering can provide the knowledge and tools to minimize the damage caused by drought and prevent people from starving, as long as the necessary money is spent. The starving and thirsty drought victims who now wander the wastelands of Africa and Asia are not the victims of cruel nature alone. They also suffer because of the miserliness of their fellow people, who have not yet learned to establish an international regime of social justice that can prevent such disasters, and who shut their eyes to others' misery. There is certainly reason to lay some responsibility for these disasters on society, on the international community. The bitter fate of starving refugees is an indirect result of being born into a world whose wealth is unjustly distributed. Most often, the suffering is the result of inaction— refraining from doing something to improve matters, at a time and in a place where action is most necessary. No, society must bear direct responsibility for the fate of war refugees, always and everywhere. Their plight is the work of humankind alone. Even a war that could justly be considered moral causes untold misery for people on both sides. So full responsibility must be attributed to society, both for the human tragedy of war refugees and for their speedy and efficient rehabilitation.

This responsibility is not only an abstract philosophical matter. There is nothing more heartrending than the sight of war refugees, paralyzed by fear, in search of a refuge from an enemy who continues to threaten their lives. Whether fleeing or living in some temporary shelter for displaced people, these refugees evoke feelings of distress. No reasonable person can react with indifference or believe these people are suffering because of divine retribution or their own wickedness. Their plight is one of the side effects of war, one of the results of the established use of violence. This fact establishes the origin of the right of refugees to rehabilitation.

N O W H E R E in the world is there a people who better know the meaning of personal, familial, and national suffering than the Jewish people. We are a nation of refugees. In our collective memory we carry the history of exile from our country, twice taken from our ancestors. We know our wanderings in Europe, Asia, and Africa; the medieval expulsions from France and England, from the German principalities and dukedoms, from Spain and Portugal. We lived with the Pale of Settlement of Czarist Russia, the badges of shame and the restrictions on employment and freedom of movement, even in those places where Jews were allowed to live; the restrictions on education and the continual humiliation, the lot of a persecuted minority. Fifty generations of pogroms and slaughter culminated in the atrocities and tortures of the Holocaust. Even before the outbreak of that terrible war, the roads of Europe were choked with Jews who had been expelled or who were seeking refuge. Jews that nobody wanted and no state was prepared to take in. Even the League of Nations committee for refugees could find no place for them, which only strengthened the Nazi resolve to carry out their monstrous Final Solution.

After World War II, Jewish refugees appeared again all over the continent, survivors of hell. With no trace left of their old towns or their families, they had no place to return to. Destitute,

they wandered the roads, with dull eyes and numbers tattooed on
their shriveled arms. Only one ancient dream gave them the
strength to endure the hardships of the journey: the dream of
returning to their ancient homeland, the place where Jews could
live a life of freedom and honor. Nobody described the emotions
of this generation better than the poet Natan Alterman. In one of
his poems, which appeared as a personal column in the newspaper *Davar,* he described the trials endured by a Jewish girl, who,
upon emerging from her hiding place on liberation day, asked
whether she was allowed to cry. "Yes, you can cry now," answers
the poet and continues:

> *The moon gazes clearly at you.*
> *The guards stand at the border.*
> *If you cross the wire fence*
> *The army and navy will pursue you.*
> *But you—you in the cotton dress,*
> *Go out alone in the heart of the night,*
> *And you walk over fields and forests,*
> *And walls crumble before you.*
> *On your compassionless back—*
> *The bundle the "Joint" gives to orphans.*
> *And in your little hand a loaf of wholewheat bread*
> *Which UNWRA provided for tomorrow . . .*
> *You will arrive some stormy night—*
> *But you will arrive! Exalted and terrible life!*
> *The laws drawn up against you*
> *Will be ripped up like the rags of your dress!*
> *Young men as bold as a fist*
> *Will bear you in their arms to the shore*
> *And your arms about their necks*

Will prevail against seventy Parliaments and the sea . . .
And between fire and the waves young men
Will stand as though dazzled
To see how, in the blink of an eye,
The first laughter will flash out of you.

Indeed, even before the establishment of the state, Israel absorbed thousands of war refugees, survivors from Europe who had traversed unimaginable routes to safe harbor and entered the area. In the official language of the time, they were called illegal immigrants. They came destitute, and the Yishuv, in spite of difficulties and poverty, took them in with love. From the moment their feet touched the soil of their people's historic homeland, they ceased to be refugees. They had a home and an identity, and a people who wanted them.

ISRAEL continued to take in refugees after the state was established. Besides absorbing people from Europe, the young, impoverished state had to welcome hundreds of thousands of Jewish refugees from Arab countries who, in the wake of Israel's 1948 War of Independence, were forced to leave the lands they had lived in. In many instances, the Jews had to abandon property that had been acquired over generations. They came to Israel, where at first they were housed in *ma'abarot*—temporary transit camps— whose conditions reflected the meager resources of the young state still recovering from the hardships of the war. It was understood, however, that the *ma'abarot* were only a temporary measure. And indeed, most of them were vacated by the 1960s, and all the immigrants who arrived during the 1950s were absorbed into the emerging Israeli society, economy, and culture.

The refugees from the 1948 war were not only Jewish. Most of the Arabs living in the regions that passed to Israeli control fled their homes, even before the state established its various institutions and the Israel Defense Forces. Since that time, Israel and the Arab states have been at loggerheads over responsibility for the creation of the Palestinian refugee problem. The Arab side claims that Israel is responsible, since it now holds the lands where these refugees lived before the war and since, they claim, Israel's forces drove these people from their homes. On its part, Israel rejects this claim, and its spokespeople lay the responsibility on Arab leaders, since they called upon the inhabitants to leave the battle zones. Their vain hope was that they would quickly win the war, wipe Israel off the map, and let the local population return. However, Arab luck did not hold: Israel won the war and the local inhabitants were left outside. Should Israel be held responsible for the fact that Arab countries did not absorb their Arab refugees in the same spirit of self-sacrifice and brotherhood that Israel displayed toward Jewish war refugees?

We could go on debating these matters, bringing proof from here and there to the end of time, but nothing will resolve the argument. (The issue has begun to interest historians, who will probably continue to argue about it into the next generation.) We need to bring the matter to a solution, so longed for from the human standpoint and so necessary from the political standpoint. As one who was close to Ben-Gurion and his generation of leaders, I know that he, as Prime Minister and Defense Minister during the War of Independence, never gave an order to expel people from their lands and homes. I have reason to believe that the Israel Defense Forces never had a "transfer" strategy. What transpired was the unplanned result of the tragic circumstances of the war, amid calls by Arab leaders to flee. About six hundred thousand Palestinians fled from Israel during the 1948 War of Independence, while we absorbed an equivalent number of Jewish refugees who fled here from the Arab countries—some six hundred thousand Jews, out of a total population of about nine hundred and forty thousand.[1] The Jewish refugees from Arab countries were immediately absorbed in Israel as full citizens with equal rights, while the Palestinian refugees were kept in refugee camps, and no state except Jordan granted them citizenship.

The leaders of the Arab countries—apart from Jordan, under the leadership of King Hussein—have chosen to prolong the refugee problem for forty-six years, while repeatedly rejecting programs to rehabilitate the refugees in their temporary dwelling places. The reasons for this were that the countries involved feared disruption and the introduction of revolutionary ideas into their lands. They also sought to use the prolonged refugee problem as political capital in their struggle against Israel. The Palestinians paid—and continue to pay—the price, and have become a nation of refugees.

TODAY, there are huge numbers of refugees again in Europe, the result of ethnic conflicts that have broken out in the wake of communism's collapse and the fall of the Soviet Union. Is it possible that these unhappy people will still be refugees forty-six years from now? Does it not seem more reasonable to suppose that they will have been absorbed and given new citizenship long before then?

Like other Israeli spokespeople from either end of the political spectrum, I can put forth numerous claims and justifications regarding this issue, in whose moral justice and logical validity I firmly believe. But who needs this argument now, and of what help could it be? Arguments and polemics may be useful for public relations, but they will not overcome the obstacles or resolve the conflicts. Personally, I do not expect the Arabs to accept our position on historical matters. Let us leave the historical polemics to the historians, while the politicians work on present-day goals, molding the present and the future. We must find a mutually agreeable, fair, and reasonable solution to the refugee problem, a solution that can be accepted by both Arabs and Israelis.

These adjectives—agreeable, fair, and reasonable—are also the foundations upon which the solution must be based. The solution must be mutually agreed upon. Something that is forced on one side cannot be considered a solution or resolution; only something that is agreed to by both parties can bring this bitter conflict to a positive and successful conclusion.

The solution must also be fair, both because it has to do justice to all concerned and because only a stable arrangement will last. To reach these two goals, the right solution cannot be unjust toward either the Palestinian refugees or the Israelis, since the wrongs of one side cannot be rectified at the expense of the rights of the other side. A solution is considered fair if both sides would accept the reverse situation—that is, if both sides were forced to change places and exchange their respective demographic features. Let us suppose that we are not concerned with Palestinian refugees but with Israeli refugees, and that demands are being made not of Israel but of a Palestinian entity. Would this entity be prepared to act according to the solution agreed on for the situation at hand? Would Israel suggest the same formula for a solution that it is putting forward now? Only affirmative answers to these questions will contain an ethical and fair solution.

Lastly, the solution must be reasonable, both because reasonableness is a precondition for fairness and because unless the solution is reasonable we will never reach a state of long-lasting stability. An unreasonable solution simply will not last. A reasonable solution is one whose formulation takes into account all the needs and pressures, all the hopes and possibilities, of all parties involved. The combination of reasonableness and fairness means that neither side leaves the negotiating room completely satisfied, but that each side knows it has gained the most it can, given the situation.

IT is hard to separate the miserable plight of the Palestinian refugees from the claim to the "right of return." For the first generation of refugees, the experience of being a refugee and the culture that grew up around it served as a basis for the consciousness of exile from the land of their birth—the loss of the country, house, lands, landscapes familiar from childhood, and family graves—alongside the hope of returning to their homes. The second and third generations have inherited this experience, a powerful emotive load that grows ever stronger amid crushing poverty and degrading conditions in the refugee camps. The claim to the "right of return" has to be seen against this complex historical background. However, it is a maximal claim; if accepted, it would wipe out the national character of the State of Israel, making the Jewish majority into a minority. Consequently, there is no chance it will be accepted, either now or in the future. No Israeli government would agree to a strategy that entailed the destruction of our national entity. In fact, the problem of the Palestinian refugees is not the only case in history where a maximal demand ruined the chances of settlement. Instead of this dead-end approach, I suggest that we look for a mutual optimum, divided into stages: the negotiation stage, the transitional stage, and the permanent settlement stage.

Even in the negotiation stage, the state of refugee camps can be considerably improved. In camps located in areas controlled by its army, Israel is ready to contribute toward improvement based on cooperation by the local inhabitants and the states involved in the multilateral negotiations. Projects such as road improvement and building renovation, installation of decent street lighting, sewage disposal, and water supply would improve the quality of life and demonstrate that full rehabilitation is not long in coming. Indeed, Israel believes that the time has come for the international agencies that deal with the refugee problem, led by the United Nations Relief and Works Agency, to look at this matter in a different light. The ideology of relief must give way to the ideology of rehabilitation. The strategy of aid must be replaced by a strategy of creating an economic infrastructure. First and foremost, refugees must be treated as human beings with consciousness and self-respect, human beings who can work and who want to take part in the development of their society and the construction of their future; they are not beggars dependent on charity but men and women who can work, think, create, and build.

A strategy of rehabilitation will preserve human dignity. This is especially necessary in the Gaza Strip, where hundreds of thousands of people lived crowded together in conditions that are intolerable at the end of the twentieth century. This is not just a matter of sanitation but also of spiritual hygiene. And it is not only a moral issue. The matter speaks to the chances for a stable peace. Continuation of the present situation in the refugee camps in the Gaza Strip, without an economic infrastructure and with below-acceptable living conditions, is a sure recipe for nationalist and religious ferment, which will end in fanatical radicalism that is opposed to peace and democracy.

Clearly, not all the necessary projects can be finished in the negotiation stage, and we all hope that this stage will not last long.

Most of the rehabilitation work and the creation of an economic infrastructure, then, will be carried out in the transitional stage. The proposed autonomy will have some real content if effort and energy are put into planning and executing a policy of rehabilitation. The quality of life can be dramatically improved for the refugees during this period of Palestinian independent governing authority, before the permanent settlement takes effect. Modern houses in planned and well-maintained neighborhoods and towns will replace the refugee camps. Indeed, there will be no more need to retain the status of "refugee," according to United Nations documents. Instead, the identity card issued by the independent governing authority will become the document that expresses the personal and national identity of the Palestinians, including refugees who live in areas controlled by the Israel Defense Forces.

FORTY-SIX years have passed since the onset of the Palestinian refugee problem, while the United Nations institutions continue to issue new refugee documents to the grandchildren of the 1948 refugees. This is part of the problematic and strange reality of the Middle East. Babies are born as refugees; but even so, there are no accurate numbers for the refugee population or data on distribution by place of residence. A definitive and official data bank is vital, not only for statistical purposes but also for planning rehabilitation, determining the level of investment needed, and setting the social and economic policies for the future Middle East. Israel has stated its readiness to help create this data bank, and will also contribute its expertise in planning for the process of refugee absorption and infrastructure construction for the refugee settlement.

The success of the negotiations and the positive atmosphere thus created will make it easier for Israel to show its goodwill in resolving the question of family reunification. In fact, since the 1950s—even before the establishment of either a transitional or a permanent settlement—it has been Israeli policy to allow family reunification, in limited numbers, on humanitarian grounds. Up to 1967, Israel had issued about forty thousand entry permits for family reunification. Since the Six-Day War, about ninety-three thousand permits for entry to the territories have been issued, also for the purpose of family reunification. But it is obvious, given Israel's security situation and the absence of a political settlement, that family reunification policies cannot be the impetus for real demographic change.

Before the permanent settlement stage, we must agree on a policy concerning family reunification. At that stage, a solution will also be found for a problem that today seems insoluble—the problem of the "right of return." As already mentioned, no Israeli government would ever agree to implementation of this right, which contradicts Israel's right of self-determination. However, once a permanent settlement has been worked out, the Israeli government should have no objection to free movement into and within the areas included in the Palestinian-Jordanian confederation. In any case, most of the refugees living in camps are already within the area to be included in the political arrangements discussed in chapter 13. Absorbing the refugees living in Lebanon who wish to move to the confederation will stabilize the internal situation in Lebanon, contributing to general stability in the region. As for the Palestinian diaspora, no Palestinian will be denied the right to enter confederation territory, just as there is no moral justice in denying any Jew's right to come to Israel.

The joint projects that will be carried out in the transitional

and permanent settlement stages will help develop the infrastructure necessary to rehabilitate the refugees. Moreover, Israel is prepared to help plan the construction of suitable housing projects
on a cooperative basis. Refugees in camps located in Arab countries will have the opportunity to relocate to new housing, while
those who settle there will have the option of owning the land
on which they will build their home. International consortiums
would handle the funding and construction of the physical infrastructure as well as the educational, religious, and health-care institutions; modern centers for industry and trade; and social
services designed to integrate the refugees into the local society.
The key concept is participation by the inhabitants themselves in
building their personal and national future.

Israel's reasons for participating in this project include establishing goodwill and the hope of reconciliation. Israeli experience
in absorbing refugees and displaced persons, especially refugees
from Arab countries, could prove invaluable to the Palestinians
when they plan and implement the rehabilitation of refugees. Perhaps this will become one of the small ironies of history.

ALMOST all peoples of the Middle East are familiar with the
problems of refugees and displaced persons, of migration, unemployment, and absorption. A regional research center could be
established to investigate all aspects of these problems, draw conclusions from the accumulated experiences in different places,
and suggest ideas appropriate to the region. A scientific research
center of this type could help immeasurably toward realizing the
peace process and establishing an economic and social policy on a
regional basis. Arab and Israeli experts would work there alongside renowned scholars from other parts of the world.

One of the traditions common to Judaism and Islam is that of scholarship. I believe that by studying our historical experience we can lay the foundation for a better future for Jews and Arabs, for Israelis and Palestinians, in this land so dear to each of us. We can wash this blood-soaked land of conflict with living water, we can grow flowers on the battlefields of the past and bring smiles to Jewish and Arab children—indeed, to all our children, who will inherit our land and live there in happiness and peace. "But the word is very nigh unto thee, in thy mouth, and in thy heart, that thou mayest do it" (Deuteronomy 30:14).

APPENDIX

Speech to the United Nations General Assembly, September 28, 1993

Mr. President:

Congratulations upon your unanimous election to preside over the 48th General Assembly of the United Nations.

We feel strongly that the time has come for all of us—communities, nations, peoples, families—to finally lay down the last collective wreath on the tombs of the fallen combatants and on the monuments of our beloved. It is the right way to honor their memories and to answer the needs of the newly born. We have to lay the foundations for a new Middle East.

The peace agreement between us and the Palestinians is not just an accord signed by political leaders. It is an ongoing, profound commitment to the next generation—Arabs and Israelis; Christians, Moslems, and Jews.

We know that it is not enough to declare an end to war. We have to try to eradicate the roots of all hostilities.

If we shall only bring violence down, but ignore misery, we may discover that we have traded one menace for another peril.

Territorial disputes may have been the reason for wars among nations. Poverty may become again the seed of violence among peoples. While signing the documents on the lawn of the White House, I could almost sense the breeze of a fresh spring, and my imagination began to wander to the skies of our land that may have become brighter to the eyes of all people, agreeing and opposing. On the lawn, you could almost hear the heavy tread of boots leaving the stage after a hundred years of hostility. You could have listened to the gentle tiptoeing of new steps making a debut in the awaiting world of peace.

Yet we couldn't depart from reality. I know that the solution to the Palestinian issue may be the key to a new beginning. But it is in no way the answer to the many needs awaiting us upon returning home.

The last decade was comprised of great changes. It saw the finale of East-West confrontation. It opened the gradual disappearance of the North-South polarization. The great continent of Asia, the picturesque continent of South America, introduced the dynamics of an economic making of their own. The dramatic event in South Africa is a great declaration to the same effect. So, contrary to all assumptions, it has been demonstrated that neither geography nor race is a harassment or an advantage to an economic promise.

We witnessed the end of some wars, only to discover that the warriors did not reach their own promised land. Some colonized people gained their independence, but they hardly enjoyed its fruits. The dangers may have been over, but their hopes evaporated. We have learned that the end of a war should be a new genesis, which will end belligerency and put an end to psychological prejudices.

No nation, rich or poor, is able nowadays to attain security unless the region in which its people live becomes secure. The scope of the regional security must exceed the range of ballistic missiles, which may hit each and all of us. We are striving to achieve comprehensive peace. No wound must remain unhealed.

Geographically speaking, we live side by side with the Jordanian kingdom, and what is so obvious geographically must become clear politically. We have agreed already with the Hashemite kingdom on many complicated issues, and there is no doubt that we can complete the story, that we can offer the people of both sides of the river full peace. The Dead Sea can become a spring of new life. The old water of the Jordan River can be a source of prosperity flowing from side to side.

We hope to—as a matter of fact, *we are determined to*—make peace with Syria. Yet we ask the Syrian leadership, if it has chosen peace, why does it refuse to meet openly? If Syria is aiming at the Egyptian fruits of peace, it must follow the process that led to it. Both of us have to look ahead and realize that the threats of war are no more than the illusion that one can return to an unbearable past.

We shall not give up our negotiations with our Lebanese neighbors. We do not have any territorial claims, nor any political pretensions concerning Lebanon. We pray, together with many Lebanese, that their country will no longer be a backyard for troublemakers. It is for Lebanon to make a choice between a Hizballah that operates from its territory and takes orders from another country, or have one army, one policy, and a real offer of tranquillity for its people and security for its neighbors. Lebanon does not need a license to regain its independence, and Lebanon should not postpone its return to a balanced policy.

Mr. President, I am not sure if there is a new order in the world, but all of us feel there is a new world awaiting an order.

We are encouraged by the new attempt of the United Nations to answer the social and economic call of the present era. The United Nations was created as a political answer. Today it must face social and economic challenges.

The Middle East, which has been an important agenda of the United Nations' history, must become prosperous, not only peaceful. To construct a modern Middle East we need wisdom, no less than financial support.

We have to rid ourselves of the costly follies of the past, and adopt the principles of modern economy. Who will and who should pay the cost of oversized armies? Who will and who should bear the price of an arms race which has reached the level of $60 billion annually? Who will and who should pay for the inefficiencies of old systems? Who will and who should compensate for outmoded censorship of mail, of trade, of travel? And who will comply with the state where suspicion intercepts the enterprising spirit of the people.

We can and should turn to the promises of scientific development, of market economy, of comprehensive education. We must base our industry, our agriculture, our services, on the height of the current technologies. We have to invest in our schools. Israel, a country of immigration, is blessed with many scientists and engineers. We shall gladly make this wealth an available contribution.

I know that there is a suspicion that when referring to a common market in the Middle East, or announcing an Israeli contribution, it may be perceived as an attempt to win preference or to establish domination. May I say sincerely, and loudly, that we did not give up territorial control to engage ourselves in economic superiority. The age of domination—political or economic—is dead. The time of cooperation is open.

As a Jew, may I say that the virtue, the essence, of our history since the time of Abraham and the Commandments of Moses has been an uncompromising opposition to any form of occupation, of domination, of discrimination.

For us, Israel is not just a territorial homeland, but a permanent, moral commitment as well.

There are other questions concerning the building of a common market in the Middle East. How do we attain this when the governments are so varied and the economies are so different? The differences in governments and economies should not prevent us from doing together what can be done together, combating the desert and offering fertility to an arid land.

The FAO declared that the Middle East must double its agricultural production in the twenty-five years to come. The population of the region in the same period will double itself, anyway. The region is cut by many and large deserts, and its water resources are stingy and scarce. Yet we know that in a similar period of time, in the twenty-five years between 1950 and 1975, Israel was able to increase its agricultural production twelvefold. During the last decade, 95 percent of the growth of our agriculture resulted from research, planning, training, and organizing.

High technology permits nations to attain real independence, and to experience genuine freedom, political as well as economic. There is nothing new about the scarcity of water in our midst. Jacob and Esau drank from the same wells, even when their paths were separated. But then, unlike today, they could not desalinate the seawater, computerize irrigation, or enjoy the potential of bio-technology.

We are meeting again with an entirely different opportunity. Greening the land can be accompanied by creating many jobs for all people in the Middle East. The most promising opportunity may be the development of tourism. No other branch of modern industry assures an immediate growth of the Middle East like this one.

Our area is blessed by nature and history, a history which is still alive: the eternity of Jerusalem, the magnificence of the Pyramids, the symbols of Luxor, the Hanging Gardens of Babylon, the Pillars of Wisdom in Baalbek, the red palaces of Petra, the inimitable charm of Marakesh, the old winds which still blow in Carthage, not ignoring the beaches of Gaza and the perfume of Jericho's fruits.

We have to open roads to those wonders and keep them safe and hospitable. Tourism depends on tranquillity and enhances tranquillity. It makes friendship a vested interest.

We have to build an infrastructure with modern means so as to dodge the chasms of the past. Modern transportation and revolutionary communications—crossing the air, covering the ground, connecting the seas—will turn geographic proximities into economic advantages. We should not ask taxpayers of other countries to finance follies of our own; we have to correct them ourselves. We do not have the moral right to ask the financing of unnecessary wars or wasteful systems.

If the thumping of hammers will replace the thunder of guns, many nations will be more than willing to extend a helping hand. They will invest in a better future. They will support the replacement of unwarranted confrontation with much-needed economic competition. Markets may serve the needs of the people no less than flags may signify their destinies. The time has come to build a Middle East for the people, and not just for the rulers.

Mr. President, it wasn't simple to open the locked doors to peace. In the name of God, let them not be closed again, so that peace will be comprehensive, embracing all issues, all countries, all generations.

We suggest that we all negotiate together as equals. We offer a common ground, made of mutual respect and mutual compromises. Thirteen years have passed since we made peace with Egypt. We are grateful to Egypt and its President for expanding understanding, identified and hidden. In a world in which so many insoluble problems reside, the Palestinians and Israelis have finally shown that, in fact, there are no insoluble problems, only people who tend to believe that many problems are insoluble.

We have negotiated one of the most complicated issues of the last hundred years. We are grateful to the United States for its support and leadership. We are grateful to both President Clinton and Secretary of State Christopher for their crucial role. We appreciate the Egyptian role and the Norwegian encouragement, the European contribution and the Asian blessing. Maybe we now have the right to say to other people in conflict: "Don't give up. Do not surrender to old obsessions and do not take fresh disappointments at face value." What we did, others can do as well.

Mr. President, we are determined to make the agreement with the Palestinians into a permanent success. Israel would consider economic success by the Palestinians as though it were its own; and I believe that a newly achieved security will serve the aspirations of the Israelis and the necessities of the Palestinians.

Gaza, after seven thousand years of suffering, can emancipate itself from want. Jericho without her fallen walls can see her gardens blossom again.

As the twentieth century comes to a close, we have learned from the United States and Russia that there are no military answers to the new military dangers, only political solutions. Successful economies are no longer a monopoly of the rich and the mighty. They represent an open invitation to every nation ready to adopt the combination of science and open-mindedness. We see at the end of this century that politics can achieve more by goodwill than by power; and that the young generation watching their televisions compare their lot with the fortunes or misfortunes of others. They see freedom, watch peace, and view prosperity in real time. They know that they can attain more if they work harder.

If we want to represent their hopes, we have to combine wise policies and regional security with market economies. Historically, we were born equal, and equally we can give birth to a new age.

"Behold, the days are coming, says the Lord, when the ploughman shall overtake the reaper, and the treader of grapes, him who sows the seeds; and the mountains shall drop sweet wine, and all the hills shall melt." [Amos 9:13.]

NOTES

1. THE DAWN OF PEACE

1. Yehezkiel Kaufman, *The History of Israeli Belief, from Antiquity to the End of the Second Temple* (Jerusalem: Bialik Institute, Dvir Publishers, 1955), p. 196.

2. AT THE CROSSROADS

1. Paul Kennedy, *Preparing for the Twenty-first Century* (New York: Random House, 1993), p. 15.

2. There is extensive literature on Islamic fundamentalism. Readers are invited to explore Emmanuel Sivan's *Radical Islam: Medieval Theology and Modern Politics* (New Haven, Conn.: Yale University Press, 1985). In *Arabic Political Myths* (Tel Aviv: Am Oved, 1988, p. 146 onward), Sivan also presents his apocalyptic forecast based on the work of the Egyptian diplomat and researcher Hussein Ahmed Amin.

3. Sivan, *Radical Islam*.

4. An academic discussion of this issue may be found in Yehezkiel Dror's *Crazy States: A Counterconventional Strategic Problem* (Lexington, Mass.: D. C. Heath & Co., 1973). Professor Dror writes not only about the types of nuclear weapons currently in the hands of these "crazy states," but also on the general behavior of, ways to cope with the challenge of the presence of, the nuclear "guerillas" of, and the unorthodox means available to such countries today.

5. Sivan, *Radical Islam*.

6. The claim was made in 1979. It was taken from the research protocol of Sivan, *Radical Islam*.

7. Ibid.

8. Ibid.

3. WAR HATH NO VICTORS

1. On the effect of this process on the concept of Israeli security and the need for the peace process, see Arye Naor, *The Handwriting on the Wall* (Tel Aviv: Edanim Publishers, 1988), pp. 77 to end.

2. Bernard Brody, *War and Politics* (New York: Macmillan, 1973), pp. 438–39.

3. Sir Thomas More, *Utopia,* Robert M. Adams, trans. (New York: W. W. Norton, 1975), p. 24.

4. THE REGIONAL SYSTEM

1. On the ultranational nature of Islamic fundamentalism as a product of pan-Islamism, see Emmanuel Sivan, *Radical Islam: Medieval Theology and Modern Politics* (New Haven, Conn.: Yale University Press, 1985), chapter 2, and the many sources he cites therein.

2. Benedict (Baruch) Spinoza, *Theological-Political Treatise,* Samuel Shirley, trans. (New York: E. J. Brill, 1911), chapter 5, section 4.

3. The literature on these issues is wide ranging, and space limitations do not allow for a complete listing of relevant sources. For a realistic summary of the political history between the two world wars, see E. H. Caar, *International Relations Between the Two World Wars* (New York: St. Martin's Press, 1969).

4. Karl Dietrich Bracher, *Die Deutsche Diktatur (The German Dictatorship)* (Köln: Verlag Kiepenheuer und Witsch, 1969), chapter 6, paragraphs 42 and 45. See particularly his criticism of the shortsightedness of the two world leaders. It follows that the problem stems from the peace-at-any-price attitude and failure to enforce the conditions of the treaty as written, not from a concept of group security per se.

5. Winston S. Churchill, *The Gathering Storm,* vol. II of *The Second World War* (Boston: Houghton Mifflin, 1948), chapter 11, subsection entitled "Hitler Strikes." Churchill quotes himself from an article he wrote on March 13, 1936.

6. *"Qui desiderat pacem, praeparet bellum,"* from Vegetius, 4th century A.D.

7. Jean-Jacques Servan-Schreiber, *The Chosen and the Choice* (Boston: Houghton Mifflin, 1988).

5. THE BASIS FOR SECURITY

1. *Polybius: The Histories,* vol. 4, W. R. Paton, trans. (New York: G. P. Putnam's Sons, 1925), pp. 389–93.

6. FROM AN ECONOMY OF STRIFE TO AN ECONOMY OF PEACE

1. As per public data sources in Israel.

2. Said el-Naggar and Mohamed el-Erian, "The Economic Implications of a Comprehensive Peace in the Middle East." In Stanley Fisher et al., eds., *The Economics of Middle East Peace* (Cambridge, Mass.: MIT Press, 1993), pp. 208–209.

3. Ishac Diwan and Nick Panpendreou, "The Peace Process and Economic Reforms in the Middle East." In Stanley Fisher et al., eds., *The Economics of Middle East Peace* (Cambridge, Mass.: MIT Press, 1993), p. 242.

4. El-Naggar and el-Erian, "Economic Implications," p. 209.

5. This estimate is based on the budgetary supplement received by the Israeli Ministry of Finance for the war (approximately $1.5 billion), not including the unavoidable cost of importing extra defense-related goods (owing to loss and erosion of equipment, etc.). In addition, there were the indirect costs of the war (channeling investments intended for other purposes into emergency security needs and a dramatic rise in the trade deficit), which hurt economic growth. For additional details, see Professor Assaf Razen's lecture, "War and Economics," in *The War in Lebanon: A View*

from 1987 (Tel Aviv: University of Tel Aviv Press and Jaffe Center for Strategic Studies, 1987), pp. 27–29.

6.   *New York Times,* April 25, 1983. Data were taken from the annual *Arab Economic Report,* published in Paris. In September 1982, the report estimated the cost of the war at a slightly lower $620 billion.

7.   See the preface to Georg Wilhelm Friedrich Hegel, *Philosophy of Rights,* T. M. Knox, trans. (New York: Oxford University Press, 1952).

8.   Hashem Aluartani, "Economic Cooperation after Autonomy: Fact and Fiction," *Ha'Ta'asiyanim Quarterly* 25 (April 1993), p. 9.

7. SOURCES OF INVESTMENT AND FUNDING

1.   Dean Acheson, *Present at the Creation: My Years in the State Department* (New York: W. W. Norton, 1969).

8. THE GREEN BELT

1.   Paul Kennedy, *Preparing for the Twenty-first Century* (New York: Random House, 1993).

2.   See Michael J. Watts, "Social Theory and Environmental Degradation." In *Desert Development: Man and Technology in Sparse Lands*, Yehuda Gradus, ed. (Norwell, Mass.: D. Reidel Publishing Co., 1985), pp. 14–32.

9. THE LIVING WATERS

1.   On the water projects in the Fertile Crescent and their effect on regional history, see Arnon Sofer, *Rivers of Fire: The Struggle for*

Water in the Middle East (Tel Aviv: Am Oved Publishers and the University of Haifa, 1992), pp. 95–96. On exploitation of the Nile, see Sofer, *Rivers,* pp. 32–35. Professor Sofer also summarizes the sources that deal with the history of day-to-day life in the river basins, and presents international legal considerations.

2.   Richard Ettinghausen, *Islamic Art and Archeology in Near Eastern Culture and Society* (Princeton, N.J.: Princeton University Press, 1951). Ettinghausen has also published additional research on Islamic culture.

3.   Sofer, *Rivers,* p. 11.

4.   Sofer, *Rivers,* p. 107 on.

5.   Data supplied by the World Bank, 1990. See also Sofer, *Rivers,* p. 119.

6.   Sofer, *Rivers,* pp. 228–29.

7.   See Jean-Jacques Rousseau, "A Discourse upon the Origin and Foundation of the Inequality Among Mankind," 1761.

8.   Sofer, *Rivers,* has a detailed discussion of the evolution of the idea of the pipeline and its advantages and disadvantages. Sofer does not accord the project much importance, claiming that it "suits the modern Western concept of cooperation between nations, advantages of growth and mutual trust, but since regional cooperation and mutual trust are not among the hallmarks of this region, the chances of realizing such a project are almost negligible" (p. 231).

9.   For a detailed discussion, see chapter 10, "The Transportation and Communications Infrastructure."

10. The Transportation and Communications Infrastructure

1. See Gil Feiler, *The Syrian Market and Possibilities for Cooperation with Israel* (Tel Aviv: Hammer Fund for Economic Cooperation in the Middle East and Tel Aviv University, 1992), p. 25.

2. Theodor Herzl, *Old New Land,* Paula Arnold, trans., (Haifa: Haifa Publishing Co., Ltd., 1960).

3. Ibid., p. 178.

4. See *Tourism Potential in the Negev during Peace* (Administration for Tourism Development in the Negev, 1993), p. 28 on.

11. The Development of Tourism

1. See the monthly survey of the Al-Ahram Institute, Cairo, August 1993, which demonstrated that the tourism industry has the most potential for development in Egypt, and is in fact the only branch of the economy that can significantly increase the country's foreign currency earnings. Development is slow, however, since Egypt must overcome two serious problems: "suppression of religious fanaticism and Islamic terror" and "the lack of peaceful relations between Israel and her neighbors."

12. The World of Tomorrow

1. Jean-Jacques Servan-Schreiber, *The Chosen and the Choice* (Boston: Houghton Mifflin, 1988).

13. CONFEDERATION

1. For the peace treaties at the end of World War I and their influ-
    ence on the creation of the troubled Middle East, see David From-
    kin, *A Peace to End All Peace* (New York: Henry Holt, 1989).

2. See Joan Peters, *From Time Immemorial: The Origins of the Arab-
    Jewish Conflict over Palestine* (Chicago: JKAP Publications, 1993),
    a book that is in full agreement with the Palestinian point of view
    in the matter of historical rights to the land.

3. For a broad historical survey of Palestinian opposition to Zionism
    and the growth of Palestinian national identity, see Yehoshua
    Porat, *The Growth of the Palestinian Arab National Movement,
    1918–1929* (Tel Aviv: Am Oved, 1976), and *From Riots to Revolt,
    1929–1939* (Tel Aviv: Am Oved, 1978).

4. See my article on the subject in the daily *Yediot Aharonot,* October
    1, 1971. A special team from the Jaffe Center for Strategic Studies
    at Tel Aviv University, which investigated the options for a peace
    settlement involving Judea, Samaria, and Gaza, included the fed-
    eral idea among the alternatives studied, and concluded that "from
    a geographical point of view this alternative is the most logical
    solution to the problem of the territories." See *Judea, Samaria and
    Gaza: Ways to a Peace Settlement* (Tel Aviv: Jaffe Center for Strate-
    gic Studies, 1989), p. 138. While the research team had reserva-
    tions about implementing this idea when the report was prepared,
    given the Jordanian government's stand at the time, on a theoreti-
    cal level, this option seemed the best to them.

14. THE REFUGEE PROBLEM

1. The number of Palestinian refugees is one of the subjects hotly disputed by Israelis and Arabs. In the absence of a trustworthy, accurate, and available source of information, there are many estimates, ranging from 520,000 (as claimed by Israel in its early years) to 900,000 (as claimed by the United Nations on behalf of the Arab countries). According to estimates by the Central Bureau of Statistics in Israel, as reported to Foreign Minister Moshe Sharett on June 2, 1949, the number of refugees was about 577,000. The bureau's conclusion is based on statistical data from the British Mandate government and the number of Arabs who remained in Israel. Since some Palestinians trickled back to Israeli territory after the cease-fire, Israel concluded that the overall number of refugees did not exceed 520,000 to 530,000. At the same time, the British estimated that the overall number of refugees was between 600,000 (according to estimates made by the research department of the Foreign Office in London) and 760,000 (the estimate of the technical committee of the "Reconciliation Committee"). As explained in the chapter, the number of refugees is important today for planning rehabilitation and development projects.

INDEX